THE YACHTING YEAR

" . . . . . the steady fore-foot snores . . . . . "

THE
YACHTING YEAR

VOLUME I : 1946-7

Edited by

ERIC C. HISCOCK

Published by

ERIC C. HISCOCK

Sole Distributors

THE ROLLS HOUSE PUBLISHING CO. LTD.

2 BREAM'S BUILDINGS, LONDON, E.C.4

THE LAUNCH

MANY a good ship lives to reach an astonishing yet graceful old age, but no matter what stormy seas she may cross or what strange shores she may visit, surely no moment in her life is quite so exciting to those who have conceived her design or wrought to fashion her, as the moment of her launch.

As the hull glides down the well greased ways, the broken bottle still hanging on the ribbons of its sling at the bows, the designer, a worried frown on his face, wonders anxiously whether his new creation will float on or above her marks, or whether some miscalculation on his part will show her up from birth to be a failure. The shipwright, his cap pushed well to the back of his head, the sweat glistening on his wrinkled brow, wonders whether those keel-bolts will hold true, and that difficult seam in the tuck of the counter prove to be sound and tight.

Not often does it happen that the designer is also the builder of the ship, but when he is, the pangs of parturition are doubled, and not until his ship has proved herself to be a good one, is he able to relax.

This new ship *The Yachting Year*, is now going down the ways. She will not be a perfect ship, for every vessel that sails the seas is a compromise in one way or another, but the cargo that she carries is the best that can be bought, and every item of it is made by men who are widely known for the soundness and the finish of their wares. This cargo is not a complete one, but all of it is new, and it contains a little bit of nearly everything the heart of the yachtsman in his winter retreat can desire.

This year has been a difficult one in which to build, launch and load a new ship. Restrictions on materials have limited her size, the threats of strikes and lockouts have hindered her building, and because of the scarcity of goods she is flying light. But year by year she will come down more nearly to her marks with an ever bigger and more complete supply of good things for the yachtsman.

E.C.H.

Printed in Great Britain by W. & J. Mackay & Co., Ltd., Chatham, and Published by Eric C. Hiscock
Sole Distributors : The Rolls House Publishing Co., Ltd.

CONTENTS

CONTENTS

A deck scene aboard the schooner *Brilliant* during the Bermuda race.

THE BERMUDA RACE

By ALFRED F. LOOMIS
Associate Editor of *Yachting*

THERE were many features of the 1946 Bermuda Race, sponsored by the Cruising Club of America, which strengthened its position as our blue ribbon yachting event—but the weather was not one of them. So it happened that the fifteenth running of this ocean racing classic was the slowest since the first, way back in 1906. It was even slower than that, for, given a breeze of wind, a modern ocean racer can sail circles in any direction around yachts of the sort that raced to Bermuda 40 years ago. The trouble was, we didn't have the wind—and that little which we did have was so consistently from the wrong quarter that the distance made good by the most favoured yachts sagged down to 60 miles a day. I mention these matters in the opening paragraph so that in this tale of the first Bermuda race since 1938 you will not look for a thrilling account of blown-out sails and broken records.

We Americans thought it was a nice gesture that gave us the R.O.R.C. yawl *Latifa* as scratch boat in a field of 34 starters. The Fife flier had met with hard luck in her 1938 try, and it was generally hoped that she would more than redeem herself in the first post-war running of our blue water classic. Loaned by Commodore Michael H. Mason, and skippered by Rear Commodore E. W. R. Peterson, who did so much during the war to gladden the stay of American yachtsmen on duty in London, *Latifa* appealed to our imaginations. But, as noted above, the weather was not suited to the British yawl's powerful hull ; and while she finished ahead of some of our own famous craft, she placed no better than sixth in the corrected order. This, I may say, seemed not to discountenance the hardy mariners who passaged her some 7,000 miles in order to race her 635 miles. They returned gaily home from Bermuda with the knowledge that their participation had still further cemented Anglo-American relationships, and with the well-founded hope that they would meet some of our loose-footed yachtsmen racing on the home course in 1947.

Speaking of gestures, there is a sloop of that name which won the Bermuda race. And *Gesture* is interesting because ocean racing is a growing, vital sport and because she was the newest product of the designing genius of Olin Stephens, who has already contributed such fast-stepping craft as *Dorade*, *Stormy Weather*, and *Zeearend*—names which are not without renown in Fastnet racing annals. *Gesture* was not, to be sure, a post-war product. She made her debut in 1941, and was then put under wraps until the evil star of Hitler had run its course. Commissioned early in the spring of 1946, she did well in preliminary races, sagged behind the leaders on the first day of the Bermuda Race, but then forged ahead to finish a good third and on corrected time to win the Bermuda Trophy by a comfortable four-hour margin.

Pursuing this same line of thought—that youth will be served in ocean racing—the second yacht to finish and to place in this long, disheartening grind was the next to the newest in Class A : the yawl *Good News*, which in 1940 looked like a world-beater. But that was the year in which the Bermuda race was cancelled because of the presence in the Atlantic of a shooting war, and *Good News* did not get her chance. And then there was the famous yawl *Baruna*, next after *Good News* in reversed order of age of the fourteen yachts in Class A. In 1938, *Baruna*, racing at the top of her class, was the world-beater. She not only finished first in the race of that year, but won the Bermuda Trophy on corrected time. She was new, she was the ultimate in ocean racing yachts. But this time she was the antepenultimate, and although her fine lines, luck, and handling again put her first across the finishing line, she settled down to third place in the corrected order.

Before forsaking this particular angle of ocean racing, let us have a look at the winner in Class B, for yachts rating less than 40. Among 19 starters, *Suluan* rated in the precise centre of the class and was the recipient of one of the special advantages of large size or of low rating. She won on corrected time and boat for boat ; she was manned by youthful dinghy sailors, and she was not only the newest boat in the fleet (with nylon sails, plywood decks, and what not) but was the first Bermuda race entry from the designing board of one of our coming architects. A. E. Luders, Jr., however, had previously turned out a class of racing yawls for the United States Naval Academy, and the new *Suluan* bears strong resemblances to this successful design. Although a newcomer among designers of ocean-going yachts, Luders has thus contributed to the development of sailing among our future admirals.

They, by the way—the Kings and Halseys and Nimitzes of the war to come—sailed two yachts in this Bermuda race, while their opposite numbers, the cadets and newly commissioned ensigns of the United States Coast Guard Academy, entered the race with two other boats. This made four service entries (which is exactly four times the

Designed by Olin Stephens and owned by A. Howard Fuller, *Gesture* won the Bermuda Trophy, the first prize in Class A, and the prize for the first sloop or cutter on corrected time.

The British yawl *Latifa*, owned and lent by Michael H. Mason, Commodore of the R.O.R.C., made a passage of 7,000 miles in order to race her 635 miles, but with light head-winds all the way, it was not her weather, and she placed sixth in the large class.

Photos : Morris Rosenfield.

total number that had ever previously raced to Bermuda) and gives me hope that in later years the fly-boys and the P.B.I. can also be inveigled into offshore racing. The United States Naval Academy didn't do too badly. With two former record holders at their disposal—the cutter *Highland Light* and the wishbone ketch *Vamarie*—they finished sixth and seventh, and placed fourth and seventh.

So far our services have acquired ocean-going yachts only by bequest or by gift from patriotic citizens (who were not, apparently, averse to casting a sidelong glance at their income tax forms) ; and it happens that the Coast Guard has not been as well favoured in its benefactions as the Navy. This partly accounts for the fact that the Coast Guard Academy schooners, *Teragram* and *Curlew*, finished and placed almost at the bottom of the list, with only a veteran schooner of the 1923 race to cushion their fall from grace. But the Coast Guard lads liked the sport and their successors at the Academy will be back for more.

One thing seeming to lead to another, I am reminded that had it not been for the Navy and Coast Guard entries, we should have been deprived of the very newest feature of ocean racing—complete air cover. Not only did a mother ship, the U.S.S. *Carpelotti*, accompany for a time and then precede the Navy racers, but on each day of the long drawn-out affair Navy or Coast Guard planes circled the fleet and reported the whereabouts of the principal contenders. Thus it came about that the sports pages of the leading metropolitan dailies were able to give a running account of the progress of the race—which was saved from being a nine-day wonder only by the timely arrival of the last boat in the middle of the eighth day. This favourable publicity, it is felt, will further stimulate interest in the sport ; and I for one shan't be surprised if two years from now twice as many competing yachts come to the starting line.

Air cover was of even more practical advantage in the case of the one racer which suffered a major casualty. This was the sloop *Flirt*, whose mast wearied of well doing (fatigue was the official diagnosis) and let go at the upper spreaders—at a spot, incidentally, where some ill-advised artisan had once placed two large bolts in the hollow spar. At the time of the dismasting there happened to be enough wind to permit further progress of the *Flirt* under an improvised jury rig. Later the motor was resorted to, and finally, when the tank was running dry, a Coast Guard plane ascertained the nature of the disabled yacht's requirements and by communication with our 99-year base at Bermuda, prompted the dispatch of a naval ship with fuel enough to get *Flirt* in.

Many years ago when it blew a succession of gales in a Fastnet race and some fifteen out of seventeen starters gave up, I gained no friends either in America or England by declaring in an article that too many boats were quitting races because of too much wind, and that despite the urgent cares of business I'd never heard of anybody who gave up for lack of wind. Time has proved me wrong, as usual. In this race, *Daphne* and *Vanda*, the only schooners in Class B, gave up because they weren't getting anywhere. But that there is a discernible difference between strong gales and Irish hurricanes is proved by the fact that these two schooners did not seek a leeward port. No, they turned on the horses and arrived in Bermuda while the festivities were still under way.

An innovation in Bermuda racing which was launched successfully this year was the starting of the small class eight hours ahead of the large class, the two groups getting under way at 9.30 in the morning and 5.30 in the afternoon. The intent was, of course, to bring the actual finishing times of the boats in the two classes closer together. Critics of the new departure claimed that light airs on the day of the start would negate the only advantage that a small boat has over a large one in handicap racing ; but as it turned out there was enough wind for both classes on June 29th, and the experiment was voted a success.

Having now covered the various angles and having already warned the patient reader that the race was unexciting, we come to the actual start of Class B off Brenton Reef Lightship in the vicinity of Newport, Rhode Island—a spot already hallowed by the races for the America's Cup in the 1930's. After the long wartime denial of such pleasures, one interested party with a tug boat anchored right on the starting line in order to command the best possible view of the proceedings. He was persuaded by the authorities to take himself hence, and the yachts went away without disorder on the starboard tack in a 10 to 12 miles per hour southwesterly. The course to the finish off St. David's Head, Bermuda, is 149° true from the lightship, and with westerly variation of 14° is approximately S. by E.$\frac{1}{2}$ E. Thus we were able to hold the course—at first.

Planes flew overhead, helping or hindering us by the slip streams from their propellers, sightseers in motor boats and sail boats did their level best to keep out of our way, and after a few hours Nature discouraged the unofficial competition by blowing in a light fog from seaward. When the fog lifted our gallery was nowhere to be seen, and from the Alden ketch *Malabar XIII*, which I had the pleasure of navigating, we had a moderately encouraging view of our rivals. The yawl *Suluan* and the sloop *Mustang*, sailed by the noted Rod Stephens, Jr., abeam and a mile or so up wind, did nothing to encourage us, but the rest of them were well astern and some were even to leeward of us. To those aboard a ketch this looked like a pretty good augury, and we promised ourselves that when the wind freed a bit and we could start the sheets we'd really show the less fortunate how to sail a race.

This happy notion brings us to 5.30 in the afternoon of June 29th when the large class started. I wasn't there, naturally, but I am told that an excursion steamer took the place of honour in the middle of the starting line and was ejected only just in time. Conditions for the start of the large class were about the same as to direction of the wind, although there was a little more heft to it, and expectations of a fast passage were rife—not to say rampant. If, now, we let 36 hours elapse, we shall have the two classes intermingled on the northerly edge of the Gulf Stream, the wind about 10 knots and all hopes high. But if it is going to haul into the southwest as we hope, or back into the south-east as predicted before the start by the omniscient United States Weather Bureau, it would better be doing it soon. Otherwise everyone aboard the 34 competing yachts will be annoyed.

Aboard *Malabar XIII* we didn't see the closest winded yachts like *Gesture*, *Good News*, and *Baruna*, pass through our class, but we did see the famous schooner *Brilliant*, which once in a trans-Atlantic passage chalked up 1,976 miles in 10 days, going like smoke hull down on our weather bow. And we saw the U.S.S. *Carpelotti* coming up from the eastward, indicating that her charges were down that way and that our position wasn't as bad as *Brilliant's* passage had made it seem. These things, as it turned out, meant nothing. Despite a new and taller rig (still gaff-headed, however) *Brilliant* sagged 200 miles to leeward of the rhumb line and was beaten to the finish by the smaller and slower *Malabar XIII*, while the Navy entries crossed many hours ahead of us.

Henry C. Taylor's *Baruna* repeated her 1938 achievement of finishing first, but dropped to third place on corrected time.

Photo : Morris Rosenfield.

With some 48 hours behind us the last of the zip went out of the wind and from then on the whole fleet struggled in the lightest of airs. To complicate the desultory proceedings, the Gulf Stream put on a show which was unbilled and no doubt unpremeditated. In its normal channel it had little if any current set to the eastward. But after the racers had passed out of the ultramarine water of the Stream and had left behind the last of the black squalls which are no good advertisement of this sultry ocean river, the current began to get in its dirty licks. Easterly sets amounting to 50 miles in 24 hours were by no means exceptional. Since at this time the wind showed tendencies of backing to the south, it may be surmised that discouragement and disgruntlement became the prevalent emotions of the frustrated racers.

In consideration of the strides made in meteorological science under the stress of war, I had really hoped that our Weather Bureau knew what it was talking about when it predicted in a long range forecast light to moderate south-westerlies, followed, in the closing hours of the race, by a south-easterly. But I didn't bank on the accuracy of the forecast as, perhaps, some less sceptical strategists did. I mean I didn't recommend to John Alden, designer and owner of *Malabar XIII*, that we continue to sag off to leeward in the confident expectation that the south-easterly would take us by the hand and lead us across the finishing line. Instead, we tacked to westward as soon as we thought we were out of the influence of the Stream and kept on doing so for 30 hours (of our total of 147 hours under way) after we discovered that not even the currents were helpful.

And we sailed and sailed until finally, hours after *Baruna* had crossed the line, we sighted the loom of Gibbs Hill Light at an estimated distance of 26 miles. From our angle to northward of the islands we were slightly nearer to St. David's Head—and, as everybody knows, twenty-odd miles is a mere nothing for a well-found ocean racer. So it was twelve hours later that we finished—to find two boats in our class and seven in the large class already in.

Despite the unflattering things I have said about the weather, it was a nice race.

Some 400 sailors, a majority of them veterans of the war, and a great many of them newcomers to the sport of ocean racing, found conditions a whole lot better than destroyer escort duty or amphibious warfare. The Royal Bermuda Yacht Club, co-sponsor of the race, was discovered (or re-discovered) to be the same hospitable rendezvous that it had been before the war.

Gesture, as has been stated, won the Bermuda Trophy for best corrected time in the fleet. She also garnered first prize in Class A, and a special prize for the first sloop or cutter on corrected time. *Good News* won second prize in Class A, and a prize for being the first yawl on corrected time. *Baruna*, as first yacht to finish, got one prize, and annexed another for placing third in Class A. First prize in Class B went to *Suluan*, second to *Mustang*, and third to the yawl *Chee Chee IV*. Schooners were not neglected in the distribution of trophies, and the famous *Nina*, winner of the trans-Atlantic race to Spain in 1928, and of that year's Fastnet race, received a prize for being the first of her rig to finish. (It is significant, by the way, that this one-time record breaker was beaten by seven newer boats.)

Then there was a prize for the best corrected time of boats built prior to 1932—the year in which the Cruising Club first developed its ocean racing rating rule—and that went to the cutter *Highland Light*. The sloop *Fun*, smallest in the fleet, was remembered with a trophy offered as a memorial to the late Thomas Fleming Day, original promoter of the Bermuda race and ardent advocate of small boat sailing. The winning navigator got a handsome silver cup, and last, but not least, the losing amateur cook became the proud possessor of a pressure cooker.

Thus a good time was had by nearly all, and the racers, having taken on stores, both dry and liquid, began the long sail home. And that, if you're still interested in the weather, was when the boys really got it. The big yawl *Escapade*, for example, blew out her storm trisail in a gale of wind, and the little sloop *Fun* was hove-to for three days with all hands below decks. Eventually the dispersed and battered fleet made home, but one and all wished mightily that in 1948 the strength of the wind will be more equally divided between the outward race and the homeward passage.

With her lee rail down the schooner *Brilliant* smokes along, but the Bermuda race was even less her weather than it was *Latifa's*, and she was placed 10th in the Class A fleet of fifteen yachts.

Photo : Frederick Bradley.

The six-metres and Q-class becalmed on the line. *Photo: Beken & Son, Cowes.*

COWES WEEK

By K. ADLARD COLES
Editor of *The Yachtsman*

THIS first Cowes Week since 1939 proved a complete success, following upon June and July, during which the number of starters at the Solent regattas had been disappointingly low. Time has been scarcer than money during the revival of yachting after the war, and the majority of owners could only race during weekends. Cowes Week, however, coinciding with August Bank Holiday and the beginning of the general holiday season, afforded racing men the opportunity to show their keenness. The number of entries in the regattas was high. For instance the combined entries for the R.Y.S. and Royal London regattas on the Tuesday exceeded 160. On that day 94 crossed the starting line, but later in the week the number of starters each day was considerably lower owing to the reluctance of owners to risk damage to their pre-war sails and gear in the stiff winds.

The fixture list followed pre-war practice. It was opened by the Royal Southampton Yacht Club on the Saturday before the official "week," following with the Royal London Yacht Club's regatta on Monday, Aug. 5th, the R.Y.S. and the R. London Y.C. on Tuesday, the R.Y.S. and the Island Sailing Club on Wednesday and Thursday, the R.Y.S. and Cowes Town regattas on Friday, and concluding with the Royal Southern Y.C. programme on the last Saturday.

Cowes harbour and roads presented as gay a scene as ever it did before the war. It is true that the Royal yacht, the "J" class, the 12-metre class and many of the largest yachts were absent, but the number of medium to large cruising yachts was perhaps greater than expected, and the small cruisers and Solent class boats were so numerous that the harbour itself was alive with hulls and sails, and it is said that there have never been more yachts to be seen lying at the sheltered end of the "Hole." The British cruiser *Birmingham* and destroyer *Obedient*, and the visiting American warships *Houston* and *Cone*, lying in the Roads, added an impressive touch to the picture, especially on Friday night when they gave searchlight displays before the fireworks started—the latter unfortunately much dampened by a deluge of rain.

The weather was kind at the start, beginning with a brilliant sunny day and light W.S.W. wind for the Royal Southampton Y.C. fixture, followed on Monday by a fog, a calm and finally a fresh breeze. Before the wind got up there was a magnificent spectacle off the R.Y.S. starting line, where class after class lay to their kedge anchors in the still water, while unanswered starting guns fired at regular intervals. At noon on that day, while the racing fleet was still becalmed, salutes of 21 guns were fired from the Squadron battery and the cruiser *Birmingham*. Not long afterwards light westerly airs broke the calm and brought the somnolent fleet to instant life. On the following days it blew hard from the S.W., making a steep breaking sea when the wind met the west running stream. Three 6-metres lost their masts ; *Caprice* on Tuesday, *Catherine* and *Kini* on Thursday. On the last Saturday a full gale was blowing for the Royal Southern fixtures. In the big handicap class only *Joyce* and *The Blue Peter* raced, and the latter was soon dismasted in a squall. In all the other classes only one yacht crossed the line and she gave up near the East Lepe, so the regatta was virtually abandoned on account of the weather. The frequency of the strong breezes during the week was unwelcome, especially in view of the poor quality of the gear of many of the competitors, but there were considerable periods of sunshine which provided a measure of compensation.

Tacto and *Draco*, two of the fleet of twelve Dragons which took part in five races during Cowes Week.

Photo: Beken & Son

So far as racing was concerned the big handicap class of cruising yachts of over 25 tons T.M. headed the racing programmes very effectively. It included some of the finest yachts afloat at the present time, such as *Joyce*, *Eostra*, *The Blue Peter*, *Firebird X*, *Kaylena*, *Cynara*, *Bloodhound*, *Old Fox* and *Nordwind*. In this class *Joyce* (P. and A. A. Fisher) took the first winning flag, defeating *Eostra* by over 40 minutes at the Royal Southampton Y.C. regatta. On the following Tuesday her topmast carried away, but on the last day of the week she had the distinction of being the only yacht to complete the course. *Bloodhound*, now owned by Patrick Egan and Lt.-Comdr. G. C. Hans Hamilton, was first at the R. London Y.C. regatta on the Monday and the R.Y.S. regatta on the Thursday, besides winning one second and one third flag. On Tuesday *Kaylena* (Kenneth H. and Brian W. Preston) had some keen racing with *Cynara* (the Marquess of Northampton) who failed to save her time. Besides being first on that day, *Kaylena* won two third flags. *Firebird X* (H. M. Crankshaw) was placed first on Friday and also won a second flag earlier in the week. *The Blue Peter* (D. W. Molins) had bad luck, for she was on the wrong side of the mark at the finish on Aug. 3rd, was disqualified on Aug. 5th and lost her mast during her sporting combat with *Joyce* on Aug. 10th.

At the R.Y.S. handicap races for 10 to 25-ton cruising yachts, *Neith* (Major G. Henderson) and *Joya* (Lt.-Col. A. W. Acland) were the most successful, *Neith* being first and *Joya* second on Aug. 8th, and *Joya* being first and *Neith* second on the following day. *Evenlode* (Chris Ratsey) won on Aug. 5th, and *Rosemary IV* (M. D. H. Wyatt) was second. *Severn* (Maj.-Gen. A. W. C. Richardson and Lt.-Col. R. H. Roome), a converted 8-metre yacht, won two thirds and *Eider* (A.E. Wood) one third.

Handicap racing for other cruisers was only provided by the R. London Y.C.

(4 to 15-ton), the Island S.C. (3 to 10 tons) and the Cowes Town Regatta (under 30-ft. L.W.L.). The first event resulted in a dead heat (most unusual in handicap racing) between *Cynthia* (Lt.-Comdr. R. M. Ritchie) and *Mary Aidan* (K. Adlard Coles) with *Shaheen*, an L 4-tonner owned by Lt.-Col. H. G. Grace, third. In the next event, for the J. Samuel White challenge cup, *Cynthia* won by two minutes over *Eider*, with *Iolaire* (C. A. W. Beaumont) third. The order in the town regatta was *Mary Aidan*, *Shaheen*, *Brunette*.

There were no " Twelves " entered, so the largest of the metre boats racing were the " Eights." In this class only *Nona* (Capt. G. E. T. Eyston) and *Rosa* (G. G. Dudley Head and J. D. C. Ewing) were racing the first two days. *Nona* won on the first two days, after which racing in this class had to be abandoned as *Nona's* owner was racing his 6-metre *Circe*. The 6-metre class was the most important at the regattas, for it was the only one augmented by a number of craft new to the Solent. Some of the best sixes had come from the Clyde to Solent owners : *Fane* (ex *Maida*, J. Dudley Head and Major Percy Garratt) *Kini* (Sydney Graham) *Circe* and *Coima* (Lt.-Col. J. E. Harrison). In addition there were two boats brand new from the yards, Sir Frank Sprigg's McGruer *Caprice* and Mr. A. J. Newman's Nicholson *Mena*. Of the older yachts there was *Nona*, owned by Mr. F. G. Mitchell, Commodore of the Royal Corinthian, *Fiona* (Norman Moore) and *Lalage* (M. Emile Hagoit). Racing was keen and not without its incidents. As mentioned before three sixes were dismasted during the week, which weakened the competition, and some close-tacking along the shore to avoid the tide resulted in many strandings which affected the results. In the first race a popular victory was won by the Belgian owned *Lalage*, with *Caprice* second and *Fane* third, a close finish with only two seconds between these last two. On the other days the results were :

Aug. 5th, 1. *Mena*, 2. *Caprice*, 3. *Nona* ; Aug. 6th, 1. *Circe*, 2. *Nona*, 3. *Mena* ; Aug. 7th, 1. *Mena*, 2. *Nona*, 3. *Kini* ; Aug. 8th, 1. *Circe*, 2. *Mena*, 3. *Lalage* ; Aug. 9th, 1. *Circe*, 2. *Fane*, 3. *Lalage*.

In the " Q " class the number which crossed the line each day was considerably less than the number entered. The first two races had the same results, *Zenith* (E. Stanley and Lt.-Col. M. Bradshaw) first, *Lintie* (H. M. Mann) second and *Flya* (Brian Neal) third. *Lintie* took four seconds during the remainder of the week, *Flya* two

Two more of the large class. *Firebird*, with her lofty new mast rising to more than 100 feet above deck, and *Old Fox*.

Photo: Beken & Son

thirds, and *Duet* (Lt.-Col. C. Bull) and *Red Angel* (J. A. C. Gaussen) one each. On Aug. 6th, 7th and 9th Mrs. H. Fulton's *Solent Gipsy* was first, a creditable record in hard weather for the oldest yacht in the class

Although five 30 sq. metre yachts raced, usually only two or three competed in each individual event. Mr. W. Janson's *Avocet* won two firsts and four seconds, Mr. H. Spurrier's *Teal* two firsts, *Hexan* (C. Desoutter) one first, one second and two thirds, *Austral* (S. H. Evershed) one first and *Alilla* (G. R. Falkiner Nuttall) one third.

The West Solent class had some very close racing, and suffered its fair share of casualties when tide-dodging in shallow water. It is said that one of these boats was knocked flat by a sudden squall near East Lepe towards the end of the week. Being in third place she was about to give up, when she found that two leaders in the class had both run aground, so she carried on with the race and won first place. *Harkaway*, sailed by the son of the owner, the late Sir James Bird, had a very successful week, winning three firsts and two thirds. Air-Commodore Quinnell's *Jade* won a place in every race, being first twice and third on the other days. *Pandora* (E. J. Coles) won a first and two second flags *Mischief* (W. Stannard) two seconds and a third.

Twelve Dragons took part in five races during the week, and produced some of the keenest racing of this year in the Solent, the difference in finishing times often being a matter of seconds. In the light airs of the beginning of the week and the strong breezes later on, the Dragons once more proved themselves to be great fun to race, and it is likely that next year will see a big increase in the strength of the class in the Solent.

Ta-Yen (J. M. S. Crean) a pre-war McGruer boat and *Lintie* (R. Preston), built in Sweden, had a close match for the best record of the week. *Ta-Yen* eventually ended up with three firsts, a second and a third to *Lintie's* two firsts and two seconds. *Peregrine*

Left :

Mistress and *Zest*, Victor Class boats, scudding bac to Cowes with mainsai reefed and spinnakers pu ing hard.

Photo : Beken & S

Right :

Bow and quarter waves an ex-six metre. A weathe side view of Mr. Gaussen *Red Angel*, racing with th Q-class.

Photo : Eric C. Hisc

(Charles Taylor) one of the new Woodnutt boats was always well up and got three thirds. *Snapper* (J. M. Sebag-Montefiore) finished second twice but withdrew on one occasion after a protest against her. *Alpette* (Earl of Hardwicke and Rt. Hon. R. S. Hudson) and *Draco* (J. Raymond) won a second and a third respectively.

The Teals fully lived up to their reputation of being consistent starters, although not a strong class numerically as yet. Capt. and Mrs. Ford's *Teal* won at the R.S.Y.C. regatta and won three second flags and one third flag during the week, but honours in the class went to *Britt* (W. W. Hughes) who secured four firsts and one second. Mr. C. E. Donne's *Content* had the bad luck to be fouled twice by other classes in the first race, and won one second and two thirds. *Zest* (Col. R. S. G. Perry) won one third.

In the Solent Sunbeam class Mr. T. Beddington's *Painted Lady* won every day except on Thursday when Major Ball's *Peggy* secured first place.

The "X" class consisted of boats from Parkstone, Itchenor and Hamble. *Silver Wind* (H. V. Culpan) won two firsts in succession and a first on Friday besides two seconds and a third. *Waxwing*, now owned by Mr. Stewart Morris and sailed with 14-ft. dinghy tactics, did very well when she got going in the second part of the week, winning two firsts and a second.

Toucan (T. Thornycroft) was the outstanding boat in the Redwing class with four firsts. *Ibis, Rosetta, Redstart, Prawn* and *Paroquet* all won place flags. An unusual incident occurred in this class on the Wednesday when all sailed the wrong course.

In the Yarmouth O. D. class *Katinka* (Mrs. C. P. W. Cross) did extremely well by gaining four firsts, while Mrs. H. W. Tobin's *Francesca* won two first, two seconds and a third. *Anthea, Genista* and *Puffin* won place flags in this class which provided some close racing. Among the Victory class boats Mr. H. H. Strides' *Zest* won two firsts, *Kingfisher* (Messrs. Glanville) and *Mistress* (Lt.-Col. W. Fellowes) and *Zena* (Dr. Murray Stuart) one each.

Taking the racing as a whole it could be regarded as excellent for the first revival of Cowes Week since the war, providing plenty of variety in sizes and classes and perhaps too much variety in the weather.

POWER CRAFT PROGRESS

A Review of Recent Motor Boating Developments.

By F. H. SNOXELL

Assistant Editor of *The Motor Boat and Yachting*

AT the time this book goes to press, Sir Malcolm Campbell is preparing for an attempt to skim the water in a motor-boat at a higher speed than anyone has achieved hitherto—faster, that is, than his own previous best, for Sir Malcolm has held the world unlimited water-speed record since 1937. In that year, with his 23-ft. hydroplane *Blue Bird*, which was designed by Fred Cooper, M.I.N.A., built by Saunders-Roe, Ltd., and driven by a Rolls-Royce engine developing about 2,000 h.p., he set up a record of 129.5 m.p.h. at Locarno, Switzerland.

Not satisfied with this, he had another boat built, *Blue Bird II*. She was designed by Commander Peter Du Cane, R.N., M.I.N.A., in conjunction with Reid Railton, with the co-operation of Adolf E. Apel, designer of the American Ventnor hydroplane, and was built by Vosper Ltd., of Portsmouth. *Blue Bird II* is a 27-ft. boat of the three-point support type. The Rolls-Royce engine from *Blue Bird* was fitted in her, and Sir Malcolm, driving her on Coniston Water, Lancashire, on 19th August, 1939, beat his previous speed by over 12 m.p.h., setting up a new record of 141.74 m.p.h.

Sir Malcolm, however, is still in a hurry. For his new attempt now in preparation, he is using the hull of *Blue Bird II*, but she is now driven by a jet engine of a type used in the latest aircraft. The success or failure of the venture will have been established by the time these lines are read.   This project has caused a flutter amongst the authorities controlling motor-boat racing and records.   Under the pre-war rules of the International Motor Yachting Union, unlimited hydroplanes were required to be driven by a propeller, or propellers, acting in or against the water.   The British delegate to the I.M.Y.U., Lieutenant-Commander Arthur Bray, proposed to the Union in 1945, the admission of boats driven by any form of propulsion.   This proposal has now been adopted.

Apart from records and racing, there would not seem to be much scope for jet motors in boats.   I refer, of course, to gas jets discharging into the atmosphere.   They are inefficient except at very high speeds and present serious difficulties in installation and weight distribution.

Water jets are another matter ;   they offer proved advantages for certain classes of craft, for instance, those operating in shallow or weed-infested waters.   In the water jet systems at present in use, the propellers—or impellers as they are usually termed—are driven by reciprocating engines just as normal propellers are driven.   The essential difference is that these impellers are installed in casings within the boat.   Water is admitted to the impellers and driven out by them through discharge orifices suitably disposed to drive the boat forward.   The water intakes may be protected by gratings, as in the widely used Hotchkiss internal-cone system.

Reverting for a moment to the rules governing record speed attempts, it is laid down that boats must not be equipped with aerofoils or hydrofoils.   Aerofoils must certainly be barred ;   it is an essential of a boat, as distinct from an aircraft, that it should be entirely waterborne.   But why should not hydrofoils be allowed, acting, as they do, entirely in the water ?

The possibilities of applying the hydrofoil principle to boats has exercised the minds of inventors off and on for many years, and many experimental craft of this type have been produced. As some readers, however, may not be acquainted with this principle, it may be of interest to mention its basic features, in view of a present revival of interest in it.

It is a well-known fact that the greater component of the lift exercised by an advancing aeroplane wing, or aerofoil, is due to the reduced pressure above its upper surface

"VS7," a German
naval hydrofoil boat,
in planing trim.

Photo: Temple Press Ltd.

the lift imparted by the increased pressure beneath its lower surface being of lesser force.

A hydrofoil boat is a craft which is designed to obtain its lift from planing surfaces which are completely immersed in the water, even at full speed. They are placed beneath the hull, to which they are attached by struts, and when the boat is in planing trim the hull itself is completely clear of the water. These planing surfaces, termed hydrofoils, act in just the same way as aeroplane wings, so that advantage is taken of the reduced pressure above them in addition to the increased pressure beneath them. Owing to the denser medium in which it works, the lifting power of a hydrofoil is very much greater than that of an aerofoil, so that, to exercise an equal lift, a correspondingly smaller area is required.

The main advantage claimed for the hydrofoil system is more speed for a given power. Admitted drawbacks are greater draught for a given size, at rest and low speeds, and greater resistance at low speeds.

During the war, the Germans carried out experiments on a considerable scale with a view to the employment of hydrofoil boats for naval operations. Some of the experimental craft are now in the hands of the Admiralty. *VS 7*, the craft illustrated, is one of these. She is 46 ft. long, with a displacement at rest of 12.8 tons, and driven by a pair of Avia engines totalling 1,500 h.p., has proved capable of a speed of 55 knots. She is fitted with a pair of stern-firing torpedo tubes.

The reports of the Germans engaged in these experiments show that many troubles and failures were encountered, and none of these hydrofoil craft seems to have been used operationally.

A British inventor, Christopher Hook, has evolved a hydrofoil system in which the foils are automatically adjusted to cope with varying sea surface conditions. A pair of antennæ, equipped with small floats at their tips, projects in front of the craft. They are articulated and connected by suitable linkage gear to the main foils, altering the angle of attack of these as necessary. That, at any rate, is the theory. Mr. Hook is at present experimenting with a craft of this type, which he terms the Hydrofin. It will be interesting to learn the result.

Although hydrofoil boats are very interesting from the technical point of view, it would seem that their scope is very limited and, like gas-jet motors, they are unlikely to influence the general trend of motor-boat design, particularly that of cruising boats, the type in which motor yachtsmen are predominantly interested.

Before turning to cruising boats, however, and while discussing developments in fast craft, mention should be made of a certain revival of interest in motor-boat racing which has taken place during 1946. The recently formed Lowestoft and Oulton Broad Motor Boat Club and the British Hydroplane Racing Club have both staged race meetings. Up to the time of writing, however, owing to extreme shortage of engines, boatbuilding materials and labour, no new racing craft had made their appearance. The boats which competed at these meetings were all pre-war.

In order to encourage racing, the former of these clubs, the L.O.B.M.B.C., has adopted a one-design craft which is intended to provide interesting racing at a reasonable cost. This boat, which is termed the Darby One-design Hydroplane, is from the board of Ivan Darby, who produced some very successful racing boats before the war. It is a single-stepper, 12 ft. 6 ins. long, and the design and specification are such that it

Two of the re-fitted pre-war boats which took part in the British Hydroplane Racing Club meetings at Bedfont Lake.
Above : A B Class Dob outboard hydroplane.
Right : A 1½-litre Whippet inboard hydroplane.

Photos : E. J. Franklin

can be constructed by a capable amateur craftsman. A standard 10 h.p. Ford car engine has been selected as the motive power, this being a model that should be fairly readily obtainable   The anticipated speed is 28–30 m.p.h. Without engine, the cost of a professionally built hull to this design should be about £110. The complete set of drawings and building instructions is available for £2 2s. from the hon. secretary of the club, Mr. C. Hildyard, Horn Hill Garage, South Lowestoft, Suffolk.

Cruising, the predominantly popular branch of the sport of motor boating, is attracting newcomers in large numbers, as is shown by the many inquiries which are being received by *The Motor Boat and Yachting*. Its practice, however, has been severely restricted during 1946 by the shortage of boats, their high cost, the difficulty of getting craft fitted out, and the miserably inadequate petrol rations allowed. From 1st August, rations were increased by 50 per cent but even so the maximum monthly allowance, 15 gallons for a boat with 20 h.p. or more, allows of only about nine hours running per month, taking the lowest figure of 20 h.p. at that. For a 10 h.p. boat the allowance is 7½ gallons, giving about the same running time. However, 1947 may prove much better in this respect. The difficulties in regard to the purchase, fitting-out and running of private boats, and the attraction of newcomers to motor cruising, have combined to make 1946 a bumper year for concerns offering cruisers for hire. Most of them were fully booked up for the season early in the spring.

None of the motor cruising " classics "—the Royal Motor Yacht Club's " London to Cowes " (actually, in the immediately pre-war years, Poole–Cherbourg–Havre–Poole, non-stop) ; the Royal Scottish Motor Yacht Club's " Field " Trophy Race, run over a 156-mile course in the Firth of Clyde ; and the " Pavillon d'Or " International Cruise—was held in 1946. I wonder how long it will be before we see a sight like that at Liége in August, 1939, when the King of the Belgians reviewed the " Pavillon d'Or " fleet in the Meuse, 86 motor yachts of all types, shapes and sizes, which had assembled by sea and inland waterway from points all over Western Europe.

Above : The 25-foot Star Craft, a Bates production.
Below : A 30-footer built by the Rampart Boatbuilding Co.   *Photos: Temple Press Ltd.*

Three of these "Pavillon d'Or" events were held before the war. In 1937 the terminal point was Paris, in 1938 Amsterdam. On every occasion British yachts formed the most numerous fleet, and took the major awards. The winner of the Liége event in 1939 was Mr. J. L. F. Stedman's 44-footer, *Scalpel II*, which had cruised 1,168 miles from Venersborg in Sweden. In the course of these events the French, the Dutch and the Belgians extended lavish hospitality to British motor yachtsmen. Surely we should organize the next "Pavillon d'Or" in this country, as soon as circumstances permit.

Unfortunately, shortage of almost everything connected with boatbuilding makes it pretty certain that motor cruising will continue to be severely restricted during the next two or three years, in contrast with the war years, during which an enormous amount of motor cruising was carried out—under the White Ensign. The shortage of boats will be eased to some extent by the conversion of some of the Coastal Forces craft into yachts.

Certain of the types now being offered for sale by the Director of Small Craft Disposals are quite suitable for this purpose. The 72-ft. Harbour Defence Motor Launches, for instance, make fine motor yachts for those who can afford to purchase and run them. The name of these H.D.M.L.s is somewhat misleading. They are quite seaworthy craft, of round bilge design, and their existing power installation and fuel capacity gives them a cruising range of about 2,000 miles at 10 knots. There is no need to change the engines, which are a pair of Diesel units totalling about 290 h.p., and are quite economical to run. They give the boat a top speed of about 12 knots. There is no necessity, moreover, to make much alteration to the existing accommodation. These boats are—or were—being sold with complete equipment at prices of round about £3,000.

The 112-ft. B Class Fairmile M.L.s, too, are quite suitable for conversion into motor yachts, but it is hardly practicable to use the original power installation—a pair of 600 h.p. Hall Scott petrol engines. In any case, nearly all these boats are being sold without the main engines. The usual price is from £500 to £600.

There are also smaller types of boat, suitable for turning into yachts, appearing in the lists of D.S.C.D.—Naval harbour launches, R.A.F. pinnaces, and ships' boats. It is estimated that at least another year will elapse before all surplus boats of the 1939-1945 war are disposed of.

Of course, many of the craft being sold are quite unsuitable for conversion into yachts, and are even poor propositions as houseboats, but people *will* try to do impossible things with them. I foresee that in a year or two many of our creeks will be littered with monstrosities which their disillusioned and impoverished owners will be only too glad to get rid of at any price.

There is at present a large and growing number of enthusiastic "converters," a good proportion of whom undoubtedly possess the tenacity and ability to carry their self-appointed tasks through to a successful conclusion. Many of them are handicapped by the difficulty of finding a suitable place where they can carry out their work. Most of the boatyards frown on—if they do not actually prohibit—activities of amateur craftsmen on their premises, but certain yards, some of them new ventures, are now specializing in offering facilities, help and advice to converters. This is a praiseworthy development. People who are so enthusiastic about getting afloat that they are prepared to spend their leisure hours for months—or years—in hard manual labour to that end, surely deserve every encouragement, as also do those concerns which provide them with the facilities for realizing their ambitions.

Although motor craft for the Services were built in such large numbers during the war, I do not foresee that what has been done in this way will have much influence on the design of post-war motor yachts and cruisers and their machinery. Even in the sphere of high speed, where one would expect to find most development, I cannot see that there has been much progress. The unfortunate lack of interest in small craft, displayed by the Admiralty between the wars, resulted in the building up of the Coastal Forces fleet—which ultimately became such a vital and valuable branch of the Navy—being a rush job, a hasty improvisation, instead of a matter of careful scientific research and forward planning. If, from the end of the 1914–1918 war, research and experiment had been officially sponsored, using the coastal craft of the day as a basis from which to progress, there would have been a very different story to tell. As it was, except for the praiseworthy pioneering efforts of two or three commercial concerns, the development of the war boat was suspended. Then, one day, it was suddenly realized that we wanted a lot of fighting motor-boats, and wanted them in a hurry.

The creation, operation and maintenance of this fleet, as all who had anything to do with it well know, caused severe headaches all round. Some of the types built had to be driven by brute force at disappointing speeds, the propulsive efficiency being very low. Some were poorly armed, and as new armaments became available, heavy weights were added to craft which had not been designed for them. The Coastal Forces fleet eventually did its job, and did it very well, but things might have been so much better and easier. Anyway, I believe that the Admiralty is now fully alive to the need for the maintenance of an efficient Coastal Force.

The German boats with which our motor craft had to contend were inferior in some ways, superior in others. Many of them were driven by excellent, high-power, light-weight Diesel engines, a type of machinery of which we sadly felt the lack. Progress is now being made in this field.

A notable achievement on our side was the creation, by pre-fabrication methods, of the vast fleet of Fairmile M.L.s and M.T.B.s. The components were made at a central factory and dispatched to many boatyards all over the country for assembly. The efficient way in which this was carried out reflected great credit on the organizers, designers, fabricators, boat builders, and all concerned.

Certain American concerns have, for many years, sold " knocked down " sets of parts for boats, and quite large craft built in Britain have been disassembled for shipment overseas.

However, this Fairmile enterprise was, I believe, the biggest of its kind ever undertaken. There would appear to be good possibilities for a similar venture in yacht production, particularly with a view to the saving of freight costs on overseas sales. Against such a scheme, it is argued that yachtsmen like to express their own individualities in their boats. But yards which have, in the past, concentrated on good standardized cruiser designs, have not usually lacked buyers for such boats. When a man buys a motor-car he is quite content, except in extremely rare cases, to accept a mass produced model.

As regards the details of hull construction, the war has been responsible for one notable advance—the increasing use of laminated construction for framing, made

Above : *Badja*, a 35-footer built by James Taylor (Chertsey), Ltd.

Right : *Badja's* wheelhouse is fitted with a comprehensive instrument panel. This is a worth-while arrangement in any motor cruiser. It helps the owner to get the best out of the machinery, and shows up defects before they become serious troubles.

Photos : Temple Press Ltd.

Below : One of the larger power yachts fitted out this year. *Eila II*, the Norman Hart designed 70-footer, slips up the Beaulieu River with very little fuss.

Photo : Eric C. Hiscock

possible by the development of efficient bonding materials, such as phenolic resin and urea resin glues or cements. This system, which saves timber and gives great strength, was adopted on an increasing scale during the later war years for the stems, keels and frames of Coastal Force craft, with excellent results.

The war also stimulated research into the use of variable pitch reversing propellers for marine craft. At present these appear to offer most scope for tugs and other commercial vessels subject to wide variations in loading, but the possibilities of their adoption for motor yachts should not be overlooked. The fixed propeller is a compromise, giving optimum efficiency only under certain conditions of loading and at a certain engine speed.

In the realm of navigational equipment, radar represents the most notable advance. The use of an up-to-date radar set largely eliminates the risks of navigation in bad visibility. Unfortunately such equipment is still very expensive. Then there is the Decca "space-pattern" navigation system, which makes position-finding and course-keeping a matter of extreme simplicity in any region served by the shore transmitters on which it depends.

The war has been responsible for introducing large numbers of young people— women as well as men, for many harbour craft were operated by the W.R.N.S.—to coastal seafaring. A big proportion of them have developed an enthusiasm for life afloat which is causing them to turn to yachting as their main leisure interest.

The day of the very large motor yachts, demanding a numerous crew and a terrific bank balance to run them, is probably closing, so far as this country is concerned—for a long time, at any rate. But there is a large demand for cruisers and yachts of moderate sizes, a demand which the boatbuilders will not be able to meet in full until the supply position becomes easier. Such post-war prototypes as have been built show no radical difference from the pre-war types, but there are some pleasing boats amongst them.

One of the most attractive I have seen in the smaller class is the 25-ft. cruiser illustrated on page 35, designed and built by Kris Cruisers (1934), Ltd., of Isleworth. This is a real good-looker and a pleasure to handle. The mistake of trying to cram too much accommodation into a small boat has been avoided. The price of this boat, which has been adopted as a standard design, is £995. This is considerably lower than that of some other boats of a similar size.

The Thornycroft plan reproduced on page 102 shows this widely experienced concern's latest design for a 42-ft. cruiser. She should be a very fine boat.

Matters to which I should like to see attention paid more generally by the motor-boat building industry in the future are insulation against machinery noise and vibration (incidentally, it is not generally realized how an ill-balanced propeller can contribute to excessive vibration ; to get the smoothest results, propellers should be dynamically balanced), the provision of open cockpit or inhabitable deck space (though many buyers seem to prefer enclosed boxes), and fresh water engine cooling systems, which not only avoid corrosion and the accumulation of excessive deposits, but enable motors to be maintained at the proper temperature for efficient running.

As the material supply position becomes easier, it is reasonable to assume that the prices of both new and used boats—which are at present out of the reach of all too many would-be buyers—will fall to a mere economic level. When that occurs, the motor-boating sport and industry can look forward to a steadily expanding future.

Photographs
of the Year

Photo: *H. S. Newcombe, F.R.P.S.*

LIQUID LIGHT
A corner of the harbour at Mousehole, Cornwall.

THREE DIFFERENT TYPES

Above : Mr. and Mrs. E. Spencer Johnson's 31-ton ketch *Escape*, built on Norwegian pilot-cutter lines. With her great beam of 14 ft. she is a powerful and roomy ship, and has been the Johnsons' floating home throughout the war.

Top left : *Teal*, one of the 30-square-metre class. Yachts such as this are usually regarded as suitable for smooth water sailing only, but during the 1946 season, one of them, Lt.-Col. Hasler's *Tre Sang*, did remarkably well in off-shore ocean racing events.

Lower left : A modern cruiser. Comdr. R.W. A. Faulkner's *Questing*, a 16-tonner designed by Messrs. Laurent Giles & Partners Ltd., and built in 1939.

Photos : Eric C. Hiscock

Photo: Eric C. Hiscoc

Above : Mr. J. Mannering's *Bird of Dawning* with her main tack triced up to a fresh breeze in the Solent.

Below : Morecombe Bay prawners at Fleetwood.

Photo: Ford Jenkins

Photo: *H. S. Newcombe, F.R.P.S.*

INCH BY INCH.—On the last of the flood the little barge yacht *Primrose* (built *circa* 1890 at Woodbridge) creeps to her mooring off Upnor, River Medway.

C

POWER CRAFT

Above : Mr. Gerald Beesly's *Mana*, designed on the lines of a Poole fishing boat, was launched in June from the yard of Messrs. R. A. Newman & Sons. Her plans appear on page 108.

Photo: Eric C. Hiscock

Left : *Saracen*, the 21-ft. fishing boat designed for himself by Mr. Nigel Warington Smyth. With her great for'ard flare and marked tumble-home aft, she is a most distinctive little vessel. Her lines appear on page 105.

Photo: Rodney Warington Smyth

Upper right : The prototype *Yachting World* 22½-ft. motor cruiser *Jenny Wren* with the Editor aboard, photographed in Gurnard Bay. This attractive little yacht was designed by Mr. Arthur C. Robb.

Photo: Eric C. Hiscock

Lower right : *Bobeli II*, the new 25-footer designed and built by Messrs. Kris Cruisers, Ltd., of Isleworth.

Photo: Temple Press, Ltd.

Right : The Atlantic, force 6.

Photo: E. A. Pye

Left : The anatomy of sails and rigging *Wanderer II*'s masthead spinnaker, and deadeyes and lanyards.

Photos : Eric C. Hiscock

Below : A deck view from the foremast of the schooner *Brilliant* during the Bermuda race. *Photo: Frederick Bradley*

LITTLE BOATS

Above : A large version of Major Wykeham-Martin's " V "-boat, which proved to be so popular among amateur builders. On the left is a close-up view of the simple leeboard, which is used in the boat with great success instead of a centreboard. It is slipped through a strap attached to the chine, and its head is lashed to the gunwale.

Photos : Eric C. Hiscock

Opposite page

Left : One of the *Yachting World* 14-ft. Restricted Class. *Merlin*, the prototype, was designed by Mr. Jack Holt.

Right : Miss K. M. Palmer's *Willow Wren*, the first of the *Yachting Monthly* 16-ft. Sharpies. The design, by Mr. J. F. d'E. Jones, is especially suitable for the inexperienced amateur builder. The plans are reproduced on page 116.

Photo : Miss K. M. Palmer

Lower : *Offcuts*, one of the Hamble River Sharpies.

Photo : H. J. Galsworthy

Bloodhound and *Joyce* racing on 6th August in the over 25-ton handicap class at Cowes. There was a strong wind and it was during this race that *Joyce* lost her topmast.

Right : The 38-foot waterline yawl *Amokura*, one of the first British yachts to visit the French coast this year, see page 60.

Photo : E. S. Harston

Below : The start of the large class in the Cowes-Dinard race. *Dodo* and *Eostra* in the lead.

Photo : Beken & Son, Cowes

SOME 1946-BUILT YACHTS

Above : Caprice stretching her sails. The new McGruer six-metre built for Sir Frank Spriggs. It will be noted that she has no upper crosstrees.

Photo: Ian G. Gilchrist, A.R.P.S.

Upper right : Firedrake, the first of the Royal Naval Sailing Association's *Meridian* Class. The plans of this 20-ft. waterline centreboarder appear on page 70.

Lower right , Saluki, Major W. M. Martineau's " long Gauntlet " built by the Lymington Shipyard. Her plans appear on page 76.

Photos : Eric C. Hiscock

Photo: Ian G. Gilchrist, A.R.P.S.

A NEW OCEAN RACER. Mr. W. Ross McLean's *Kelana* was designed and built by McGruer. Here she is seen beating down the Gareloch in a fresh breeze. A most distinctive feature is her great forward sheer.

Opposite page : Dyarchy, the 27-ton gaff cutter owned by Roger Pinckney, Vice-Commodore of the Royal Cruising Club. Designed by Laurent Giles & Partners, this fine ship was built in Sweden by S. Truedson in 1939.

Above : The 5-ton cutter Anthony at Cherry Garden pier. After an Estuary cruise her mast has been lowered prior to going up river.

Right : The forest of masts that is Burnham.

Photos: H. S. Newcombe, F.R.P.S.

45

Above : *Mary Aidan* has trouble with her spinnaker. The design for this yacht, by Mr. F. R. Parker, won a prize in a competition held by *The Yachtsman*, and appears on page 86.

Photo: Eric C. Hiscock

Opposite page : Two new Thornycroft yachts : *Fidalga II*, Mr. K. C. Barnaby's 18-ton motor sailing cruiser (for plans see page 100) and *Mona*, a 52-foot fast Diesel engined cruiser built for H. E. Ahmed Abboud Pasha (see page 104).

Photos : John I. Thornycroft & Co., Ltd.

MOONRAKER SAILS TO SOUTH-WEST IRELAND

By E. A. PYE

MOONRAKER is a ten-ton auxiliary gaff cutter. We found her in Polperro some fourteen years ago and had her converted into a comfortable ship for my wife and myself to sail on our own.

This year we wanted to go to South-West Ireland, so we decided to sail her down to Helford at the beginning of April and leave her there till the end of June, when we hoped to continue our voyage.

For the first time since we bought her, we asked a friend to come with us for six days, to lighten the work and hasten the voyage ; so *Moonraker* sailed from Burnham on Thursday, 4th April and dropped anchor in Dartmouth harbour on Sunday evening, four days and three nights out from the Crouch. From there Anne and I sailed on westwards, visiting Fowey and St. Mawes before leaving her on *Tern IV's* mooring in the Helford river.

Encouraged by the success of having a third on board, we asked two friends to come with us to Ireland.

On Friday, 28th June, *Moonraker* followed *Wanderer II* out of Helford river bound for the Scillies, but had to put into Newlyn as all her crew were sick. The next day we left again in *Wanderer's* company, bound once more for the Scillies, but luck was against us that trip. Although we drove the ship for all she was worth, we failed to weather the Seven Stones and found ourselves to the north of the light and whistle buoy.

The passage so far had been uncomfortable, to say the least of it ; the seas were big and spray came over in sheets, and two or three times a sea broke over the lee rail flooding the cockpit while the top of another one would come over the weather bow. Our friends dare not go below, and they were not equipped for off-shore cruising, having no proper oilies or sea boots. There was no alternative to their being soaked above, or sick below.

Off the Seven Stones we tacked ship and hove-to to put in a couple of reefs. Unfortunately the jib took charge while being lowered, and the block, flogging against the port crosstree, brought it hurtling to the deck. Four hours later *Moonraker* sailed back into Newlyn harbour, to lick her wounds and change her crew.

No sooner had we berthed than a friendly shipwright came aboard to see if he could help us. He promised us our new crosstrees by Monday afternoon. On the Sunday morning I put in some hard work on the long distance telephone and was lucky enough to get hold of Daphne French of the Irish Cruising Club. She left London that night and we met her at Penzance the next morning. All that day the ship was a

Illustrations on opposite page :—

Top left : Dunkerron Islands in the Kenmare River.
Top right : Gascanane Sound, between Sherkin Island and Cape Clear.

Centre left : *Moonraker* leaving Glandore.
Centre right : Approach to Glengariff.
Lower left : Horseshoe Harbour.
Lower right : Glandore.

Photos : E. A. Pye.

hive of terrific activity, the shipwright up aloft fitting the crosstrees, Anne patching
the mainsail in two small places, the sailmaker measuring us for a new mainsail for next
year, and the old crew and the new working at all the odds and ends that must be
done before putting to sea.

On Tuesday morning *Moonraker* sailed once more in a light wind from S.S.W.
and lay close-hauled out of Mounts Bay, bound for South-West Ireland. An hour
after leaving Newlyn a thick mist descended on us and we saw neither Runnelstone
buoy, Land's End nor Longships the rest of that day. We sailed over a quiet sea in light
airs, or used the engine when these failed, but at 7.30 p.m. the mist cleared as if by magic
and there was the Seven Stones whistle buoy, broad on the port bow.

The wind left us at sunset, and we lay becalmed all night. We took the topsail off
her, hauled the mainsheet hard in, and went to sleep.

I got a fix before dawn putting us seven miles north of Round Island light and from
this we took our departure when a breeze came up from the east an hour later.   Up
went the topsail, and the big reaching jib was set as a spinnaker using the squaresail
yard as a boom. The main boom had to be guyed forward with the handy-billy as
the wind was too light at first to keep the sail asleep. The watch below had to sit on
the spinnaker boom to keep that quiet as well.

For the next twelve hours we ran before the wind on a N.W. course. The heavens
opened, the rain came down in torrents and the glass fell steadily.   Then the
wind veered in a sudden squall to S.S.E. We got the topsail off her and put in a couple
of reefs, setting the No. 2 jib. Everything pointed to its being a dirty night at sea, but
to our surprise, the wind dropped at sunset and we lay becalmed once more. The
reefed mainsail was sheeted in and the ship's company retired to sleep. The glass had
fallen four-tenths in twenty-four hours. The dawn next morning was fiery red, but the
rain had ceased. The glass was inclined to rise and the wind came in from the east.

Soon the character of the morning changed. Rain squalls swept across the sky,
the wind veered rapidly to W.S.W., and *Moonraker* lay close-hauled to an ever increasing wind and sea. Just as we finished lunch, I saw a wild-looking squall bearing
down on us. I called all hands and we got the jib off her just in time and reefed the
mainsail well down.

The squall passed, but the wind freshened again ; the foresail was reefed and then
taken off. Despite her small sail *Moonraker* was getting very wet and life below decks
became a bit difficult. Daphne injured her knee, and Anne, at the helm, had her tea
laced with salt water on two occasions before she had time to drink it. The wind
veered to W.N.W. and the cross swell wanted watching carefully. Finally we set the
reefed foresail, took the jib off her and hove-to.

Dinner that night was an austere meal : " tiller soup," biscuits and coffee. Daphne
had her mattress on the cabin floor, Anne and I dossed down head to tail on the lee
bunk. From time to time I looked out on the tumbling waste of water and at midnight
I sailed her for an hour on a course just east of north. But it was soon blowing as hard
as ever and I hove her to and retired below. The crew, more wisely, had remained where
they were.

At 5.45 a.m. all hands turned out. No. 2 jib was set and we resumed our voyage.
Course N. 10° W., wind W.N.W. fresh to strong, log 107, and a bright fine morning.
The barometer had risen three and a half tenths.

Later the reef came out of the foresail and I began to think of a landfall. I reckoned that on our course we should make the Old Head of Kinsale, but I didn't think we should see anything before noon ; at 10 o'clock, however, I saw land on the starboard bow and an hour later this appeared as a bold headland with land running away to the N.E. to the right of it and N.W. to the left. For one awful moment I thought I was fifty miles out of my reckoning and that we were sailing for Mizzen Head ; but there was no Fastnet rock to be seen, and presently more land appeared on the port hand, curving south-westwards, forming a large bay.

We had a grand sail that morning, the old ship doing a good 5 knots with the mainsheet a little eased, and at noon the Old Head bore N.W. distant 3 miles. As we closed with the land, the sea went down and we altered course to N. by W. for the harbour entrance. What fun it was, this first landfall in a strange country. We ran on, past a tiny cove on the starboard hand with two or three whitewashed cottages and a boat pulled up on its sandy beach. Then a sharp bend to port and the old town of Kinsale came into sight across a wide stretch of water : a perfect land locked anchorage. We dropped our hook off the Customs Quay.

While Anne and I tidied up the ship, Daphne went ashore in the pram, to return with four pints of milk, two loaves of bread, raspberries, cream, a pound of butter and a promise of baths at Actons Hotel. We had indeed arrived in the land of plenty.

We shopped and dined and laughed in this sleepy delightful town where people always smiled and were so polite and helpful. Then, at 11 o'clock the next evening we sailed out before a light northerly air.

The hills and valleys were bathed in moonlight, and as we passed our little cove, sounds of a haunting Irish tune floated across the water. A most romantic scene.

Off the Old Head of Kinsale we lay becalmed till after breakfast ; then a breeze came up from the west and we beat down the coast in brilliant sunshine, past the Seven Heads and Galley Head, from which we could see the bold headland that forms the

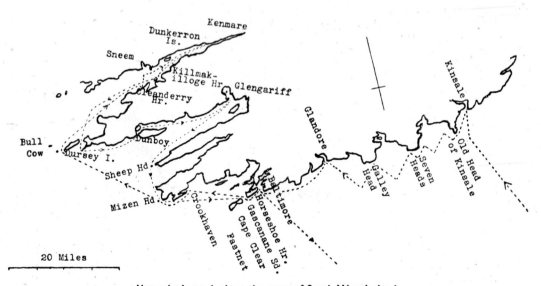

Moonraker's track along the coast of South-West Ireland.

east side of the entrance to Glandore Harbour. High and Rabbit Islands to the west-ward helped to confirm its position.

The wind failed as we reached the entrance and we motored in past Adam Island, but in the dusk we missed Eve until the perches, marking the rocks in the centre, showed up dead ahead. We turned sharply to port and there was Eve, dark against the shore. After all, she is only twenty-five feet high! In the perfect calm of a summer night, we dropped anchor in two fathoms off Glandore village, and so to bed.

The next morning no vestige of breeze troubled the waters of this lovely anchorage. A tiny inner harbour lay at the foot of the village and white cottages lined the single street which winds up the hillside. In the afternoon we sailed up to Union Hall at the head of the harbour, but the place seemed rather dirty and unattractive. Anne and I climbed up the hill above the village and had a glorious view of the mountains in the west.

We sailed for Baltimore on the Wednesday. It took us twelve hours to make the eighteen miles and even then we had to motor into the harbour in a dead calm. Alber the porpoise or whale piloted us in, but we did not see him as we left two hours later to motor into Horseshoe Harbour, a charming little anchorage on Sherkin Island.

No wind the next day; so after tea we motored through Gascanane Sound and laid a course for Crookhaven, arriving at 9.30 p.m. A perfect day for sightseeing as there was hardly a cloud in the sky and the mountains stood out in bold relief. Long Island Bay looked most attractive and we wished for more time to explore the fascinating waters between Mizzen Head and Cape Clear.

The tide round Mizzen Head meant an early start the next morning, but once round that mighty headland we felt a breeze, no, an air, from S.W. The topsail and big reaching jib were soon aloft, but it never strengthened above force 2, and we meandered past Dunmanus and Bantry Bays and past Dursey Head, inside the Bull and Calf and then eastwards, with a light west wind, following the southern shore of the Kenmare river. Anne had been studying the chart intently.

" What about Cleanderry Harbour, with its 25-foot entrance ? " she asked.

So we hugged the shore, passed Yellow Island and came in sight of the tiny opening. We seemed to sail down hill into a landlocked lagoon, and brought up in ten feet (low water), close to the weather shore. Outside one heard the whisper of the surf breaking on the rocks, inside it was so calm and still that the moon's reflection lay unruffled on the water's surface.

For the first time for a week we woke to the sound of wind in the rigging. A fresh N.W. breeze was blowing across the river and most of the higher mountains were hidden in clouds. After exploring Cleanderry and going ashore for milk and potatoes, we got under way and lay close-hauled out of the narrow entrance and beat over towards Sneem, but this did not attract us very much, so we turned and ran up the river. We towed the pram, as there was no sea to speak of. The scenery was grand. We anchored a mile west of the stone quay which serves as a little harbour for Kenmare and went ashore. Our shopping expedition to this little country town was most satisfactory and we returned well laden to the quay ; but the whole scene had changed in that short time. The wind had backed to W., and was blowing quite hard. The tide was ebbing and we had a very wet pull back to *Moonraker*, Daphne and I at the oars and Anne baling for all she was worth. After tea we put a reef in the mainsail and set the No. 2 jib, but it came on to rain and the visibility was very poor, so we went no farther than the Dunkerron Islands, and anchored in their lee.

Sunday, 14th July, was a red-letter day. We woke at 5.30 to a fine sunny morning with a W.N.W. breeze and a rising glass. We beat down the river and ran into Killmakilloge, anchoring for breakfast in Collorous Harbour. Afterwards we went ashore and took some photographs, drank milk at a cottage and returned on board to get under way once more. We beat out of the harbour, took a long board across the river and found that we could lay our course out to sea, but the wind was now fresh and we put in a reef.

The south-going stream through Dursey Sound started at 3 p.m., and half an hour later we were off the entrance making for this gap between the cliffs before a big sea and a following wind. It was an awe-inspiring sight watching the sea breaking on the rocks a few yards away, and we wondered whether *Moonraker* would gybe all standing as she entered the sound. There was a confused bumpy sea at the entrance and then we were inside tearing along with the fierce spring tide under us. The rock in the middle of the narrows gave us no anxiety; the tide rip over it could be clearly seen and we hugged the Dursey Island shore. Round the corner we kept to the starboard side out of the tide rips and then gybed round Crow Head at a distance of half a mile.

With the fresh off-shore wind *Moonraker* raced up Bantry Bay burying her rail in the squalls. Off Black Head I had to give Anne a hand with the tiller in a fierce puff, and we looked anxiously at our mast, but we carried on with our one reef and arrived safe and sound in Dunboy Bay after a really glorious sail. We stayed in this delightful anchorage all day on Monday while it rained bucketsfull and a thick mist blotted out everything over a mile way. Daphne even said that she woke in the middle of the night and heard the castle ghost gurgling in the water.

On Tuesday, the day we ought by rights to have turned towards England, we sailed before a light west wind to Glengariff. The approach to that famous harbour is indeed lovely, but it was too touristy for our simple tastes, and we had an indifferent meal at Eccles Hotel. Mr. Peverly of the R.C.C. came aboard after dinner and we had a very entertaining evening.

The next morning we lay close-hauled out of Bantry Bay to a fine sailing breeze from N.W. The crew cast longing glances at Dunmanus Bay and quoted Eric Hiscock to me, but I spoke sternly to them and reminded them of the call to duty. They were not impressed, so, just to make quite sure, I sailed the ship myself until we were past Mizzen Head.

From there we laid a course to Gascanane Sound, but off Crookhaven I saw a squall come tearing across the bay churning the water into a sheet of foam. Down came the jib, just in time, and we took three reefs in the mainsail while the wind fairly shrieked in the rigging. In a few minutes the whole thing was over and we were back on our course with our full sail; and then the landsman asks you how you get your exercise when you are sailing.

As we approached the northern end of Cape Clear another squall appeared and we put two reefs in, but this time nothing much came of it, and we ran comfortably before a hard breeze through Gascanane Sound and round into Horseshoe Harbour.

Thursday, 18th July. This morning we were sad, for tonight we must leave this delightful country, untouched by war, where there is a gaiety of spirit and a contentment in the simple pleasures of life which exists no longer in the towns and cities of England.

We left Horseshoe Harbour with a reef in the mainsail and sailed into Baltimore, anchoring off the village. There we filled our tanks from our canvas water breakers, visited a shipyard where they were building a twenty-five tonner, and took in bread and last-minute stores. I talked to some fishermen on the quay before going aboard. They had just come in and told me that there was plenty of wind outside with a big swell five miles off the land. It was certainly blowing freshly inside the harbour and I reckoned that if this held, we should pick up Pendeen and Round Island lights before dawn on Saturday.

We dined well that evening and then set about preparing the ship for sea. We put a second reef in the mainsail and hove up the anchor just as the lights were appearing in the cottage windows ashore. We took a couple of tacks towards the Lousy rocks, then ran for the entrance escorted by Albert.

We streamed the log off the Loo buoy and set the course S. 40° E. My last fix was at 1 a.m. and put us 13½ miles S. 50° W. of Galley Head, the log reading 11. There was now quite a big swell running and the old ship rolled her way merrily along, averaging just over 5 knots, and very comfortable she was too, under her shortened canvas.

After breakfast we set the topsail over the reefed mainsail and we rolled along a little faster and just as comfortably. The wind was W. or W.N.W. fresh. Two-hour watches were kept day and night as is the practice on board this ship when passsage making. The sun came out just in time to get a meridian altitude which put us eight miles south of our dead reckoning.

At 6.30 p.m., the log reading 101, I altered course to S. 55° E. which would take us well clear to the north of the Seven Stones. We were then running dead before the wind and we set the squaresail; for a couple of hours *Moonraker* fairly roared along, rolling heavily, dipping the end of her boom into a sea occasionally, picking up a little water with her lee rail and chucking it playfully across her bridge-deck out into the sea again, as she rolled to starboard. She logged just over twelve miles in that watch.

Daphne was at the helm when we sighted a sail away to starboard, the first yacht we had seen for nineteen days. She crossed our bow close-hauled on the port tack, sailing well under trysail and staysail.

The squaresail and topsail came down before dinner, as we wanted our meal in comfort and the wind was freshening. As it grew dark we saw three steamers in quick succession on a S.W. course some four or five miles ahead of us, and at 11.30 p.m. we picked up the loom of Pendeen light fine on the starboard bow, and I altered course again to S. 40° E. During the night I took frequent cross bearings, but we never saw the Seven Stones light and whistle buoy.

Then, just as we were beginning to think of Newlyn for breakfast, the wind dropped leaving us becalmed off the Longships; and that was misery. We sheeted in the mainsail and for three solid hours *Moonraker* rolled her rail under in a persistent fiendish way. I have never cooked breakfast before in such trying circumstances and neither Daphne nor Anne could risk the cabin for more than a few minutes. Afterwards I started on the engine, but this for once would not go; water had been sucked through the exhaust pipe. But after a bitter struggle, it started. Then a breeze came up from the west and we were soon running up the coast with the topsail set and all our troubles forgotten. At 12.30 p.m. we rounded-to off the entrance to Newlyn, got the sails off her and motored into the harbour, thirty-eight hours out from Baltimore.

When the customs came aboard we were all sound asleep with the lunch things still on the table, but one by one we recovered consciousness and in due course the ship was cleared.

As I came up on deck I saw a blue yawl anchored near the entrance. No one could fail to recognize her so often has her picture been drawn by Robert E. Groves.

"She's just come over from Cape Clear," said the Customs, "Mr. O'Keeffe left early on Friday morning."

Paddy O'Keeffe came over our transom at breakfast time next morning, and in a moment we felt we had known him all our lives. He told us stirring tales of battles long ago ; how the O'Sullivans sacked Baltimore and how Cape Clear was a Christian community while Eire still lay under the dark cloud of barbarism.

We listened spellbound to our visitor who weaved such magic into bygone days. As he rose to leave, I asked him, hesitantly, whether he ever came to London, and would he come and see us.

" I should be lost in your great city," he replied, " I am a man of the mountains and the sea."

We watched him row back to his ship, sad indeed that his way of life was not ours ; and that our voyage to his romantic land was over.

BLUENOSE
1921—1946

By BEVIL WARINGTON SMYTH

IN the spring of 1921, there was launched at the yard of Smith and Ruhland at Lunenburg, Nova Scotia, a fishing vessel that was destined not only to become famous in her own country but to achieve international renown. This was the schooner *Bluenose*, one of the last of that great fleet of sailing fishermen hailing from New England and Nova Scotian ports, which worked the offshore banks from Georges Shoals to the Grand Banks of Newfoundland.

Bluenose was designed by W. J. Roue of Halifax, N.S., for Captain Angus Walters and partners. She measured 141 feet on deck, with a waterline length of 112 feet and a beam of 27 feet, and drew nearly 16 feet of water. Her rig was the conventional Banks schooner rig, namely, jib, jumbo, fore and main, with gaff topsails on both masts, a big jib topsail (known as the balloon) and that fine driving sail the fisherman's staysail. She had the long graceful overhangs and sweeping sheer customary in the later models of Banks fishermen. The profile of her bow was distinctive, there being a rather sudden turn to the curve of the stem before it ran down into the straight line of the long sloping forefoot. The counter stern was finished off in a beautifully modelled elliptical transom—typical of many New England and Nova Scotian craft.

The year before *Bluenose* was launched, the schooner *Esperanto* of Gloucester, Mass., had won the first official international fisherman's race from the Nova Scotian schooner *Delawanna*, and it was with high hopes that the Lunenburgers looked to *Bluenose* to avenge this defeat and win the Dennis trophy for Nova Scotia. This she had no difficulty in doing, for the American defender in 1921 was the little *Elsie*—an able vessel and superbly sailed—but no match for the big new salt banker.

In the following year, 1922, *Bluenose* sailed to Gloucester to defend her title. The Americans, meanwhile, had built two potential challengers, the *Mayflower* of Boston and the *Henry Ford* of Gloucester. The *Mayflower*, designed by Starling Burgess, was a big vessel 143 feet over all and 112 feet on the waterline, with a beam of 25.8 feet and a draught of 16 feet. She was debarred from the race, however, on the grounds that she had been built more as a yacht than as a fisherman—an allegation that seems difficult to follow, as the vessel subsequently fished out of Boston, both winter and summer, for many years. There seems to be little doubt that she was a faster vessel than *Bluenose*, if not the fastest two-masted fisherman ever built, judging by the performance she put up in an exhibition sail round the Cup Race course.

As a result of the *Mayflower's* disqualification, the *Henry Ford* of Gloucester became challenger in 1922. She was a big fast vessel and was cleverly handled by her skipper, Captain Clayton Morrissey, but she was not quite fast enough to win the Cup from *Bluenose*.

These fishermen's races accentuated the spirit of intense rivalry which existed between the New England and Nova Scotian fishermen, and led on more than one occasion to serious disputes and bitter feeling. This rivalry was due largely no doubt to patriotic sentiment, but it also sprang from the intense pride which these fishermen had in their vessels.

The failure of the *Henry Ford* to wrest the cup from *Bluenose* came as a great disappointment to Gloucestermen. But the following year, 1923, a vessel was launched from the yard of Arthur Story which is said by many to have been the fastest schooner ever launched from a Gloucester yard. This was the beautiful *Columbia*. Like *Mayflower*, she was designed by Starling Burgess, but whether she was really faster than the Boston vessel is problematical. On a reach, in a strong breeze, this wonderful schooner was capable of a speed of over 16 knots. Captain Ben Pine, her skipper undoubtedly got the best out of her when she defeated *Bluenose* off Halifax that year in two straight races. But, as usual, the series was marred by a dispute which resulted in *Bluenose* being disqualified. Captain Pine had then only to sail over the course to win the trophy but this he declined to do. The two vessels never met again, as not long afterwards the beautiful *Columbia* was lost with all hands.

Bluenose's next opponent was the *Gertrude L. Thebaud*, designed by Frank C. Paine of Boston. She was another handsome, yacht-like vessel—a distinctive feature of her sail plan being the higher peak given to her mainsail than was customary in a fisherman. In 1930, at Gloucester, she beat *Bluenose* in two straight races, but on this occasion the Dennis Trophy was not at stake. The following year, off Halifax, *Bluenose* defended her title successfully by defeating *Thebaud* in three straight races. By this time she was getting on in years, as age is reckoned in a Banks fishing schooner, and her performance in defeating the speedy *Thebaud* must be considered a fine one. It should be remembered, however, in *Thebaud's* favour that she was a smaller vessel, her waterline length being just under 100 feet as compared with the 112 feet of *Bluenose*.

Bluenose, from an ink sketch by the author.

The two vessels met for the last time in 1938. The racing was again marred by acrimonious disputes. Each vessel won two races, and the fifth and final race of the series went to *Bluenose*, who thus retained her championship title.

But these periods of racing were after all but brief interludes in the life of the big schooner. She was first and foremost a fisherman, and year after year she earned her living on the Banks—a hard and perilous calling. The dangers attendant on fishing from dories in winter time, with the vessel anchored in shoal water or jogging along under shortened canvas, can be realised when one considers the number of schooners that sailed forth on a fishing trip and never came back. For example, of the vessels mentioned in this article, the *Esperanto, Henry Ford, Elsie* and *Columbia* were all lost.

Bluenose herself narrowly escaped a similar fate on one occasion when she was caught at anchor off the north west bar of Sable Island in an onshore gale. It was not long before the cable parted and she was adrift on a lee shore in one of the deadliest patches of shoal water in the world. Only a sailor can fully appreciate the terrible nature of her predicament. The reefed foresail and jumbo were set and Captain Walters, lashed to the wheel, headed the schooner away on the port tack, hoping that the wind would stay long enough in the south-west to enable her to work clear of the north-west bar. But after a few hours the wind began veering more to the westward. This brought disaster very near. Captain Walters was now obliged to get on the other tack at all costs. It took time to wear ship and every second of that time the vessel was driving into shoaler water, running at a great pace before the squalls of sleet and snow. By the time the schooner had been brought to the wind again on the starboard tack, the seas breaking over her were yellow and gritty with sand. It was touch and go for a long while, and then the wind veered a few points and she was safe. She did not, however, come out of the ordeal unscathed. Her decks were clean swept of everything movable and she sustained much damage besides to bulwarks, stanchions and rail.

In 1935, *Bluenose* sailed across the Atlantic and up Channel to Spithead where she took her place amidst the great fleet of shipping assembled for the King's Jubilee review. The famous fishing schooner cruised in Solent waters for some weeks and attracted a good deal of attention. Later in the summer she sailed to Torquay and Plymouth and then on to Falmouth, where she arrived at the end of August. Here preparations were made for the return passage across the Atlantic.

She sailed from Falmouth at noon on Wednesday, September 12th, bound for Halifax. In addition to her crew, which consisted of captain, mate, four hands and four boys, there were ten passengers on board. Under her four lowers, the schooner beat down to the Lizard against a fresh S.E. by S. breeze.

As she opened the western land she came into a heavy swell from the westward. This, combined with the easterly sea, made things very uncomfortable. At 5 p.m. the captain gave orders to stow the mainsail. The ship was rounded up into the wind and the 84 foot boom lowered into the crutch and secured with tackles and chains. The big sail was lowered and furled and the riding sail set in its place. Course was then set to pass some 25 miles south of the Bishop. Without the mainsail, and in the confused sea running, progress was very slow.

On the following day, the schooner being then something to the south and west of the Scillies, the wind came ahead and freshened to half a gale. The jib was stowed and triced up on the stay. By midnight the wind had increased to a gale and Captain Walters wore ship and stood S.S.W.

It continued to blow hard on the two following days, Friday and Saturday, with the ship making very little progress to the westward. The vessel was labouring heavily and a persistent leak which had been prevalent for some time had now increased so that it was taking 140 strokes of the pump every hour to free her. *Bluenose* would not lie-to quietly under such short canvas. She kept ranging about and, while her head went into the sea easily enough, her counter pounded badly.

On Friday afternoon a topsail schooner was sighted about 4 miles to the southward running for the Channel. She was carrying two jibs, lower topsail, boom foresail and double reefed mainsail and was travelling fast.

On the Saturday, towards midnight, a terrific squall struck the vessel. It smashed the fore gaff short off about 15 feet from the jaws. Luckily the sail was a brand new one and it was got down without any damage. *Bluenose* now had only the jumbo and riding sail set, and the pounding of the counter became worse than ever.

The next day, Sunday, there was rather less wind but it was still dead ahead.

Monday, September 16th, broke with a low sunrise, which some thought was a sign of better weather, but there was a very brilliant green eye in the sky to the eastward out of which the sun rose above the water. Just before this, a large mass of black clouds banked up to the northward gave every appearance of a shift of wind, but nothing came of it and it continued to blow from the west.

At daylight a sail came in sight to leeward which was made out to be a French tunnyman. She was close-hauled on the port tack, heading about N.W. and bounding along gaily under well reefed mainsail and small jib.

At 7 a.m. all hands were turned-to to fish the gaff. The ship was then on the starboard tack heading S.S.W. Soon after, it came on a deluge of rain. This eased about noon but the wind had by now increased to a heavy gale. At 1 o'clock the sky cleared away and the wind settled due west and blew with hurricane force. The jumbo had been lowered sometime before ; now the riding sail was reefed. Even this was too much, so it was lowered till there were only about 12 feet of luff above the main-boom.

All afternoon the sun shone brightly in a cloudless sky. The tops of the seas were blown into a solid bank of spindrift which drove along 30 or 40 feet above the water.

The hurricane reached its height at about 6 p.m. (a velocity of 98 m.p.h. was recorded at the Scillies). About 11 p.m. a very heavy sea broke aboard the vessel, throwing her almost on her beam ends and smashing the two boats, the foreboom and the jaws of the mainboom. The ship went down to a considerable angle but righted quickly. The two men at the pump were washed overboard, but having life-lines on, managed to haul themselves back on board. From now on the leak began getting worse, and the pumps had to be kept going almost continuously.

At midnight, all hands went below to shift ballast in an effort to locate the leak which was clearly somewhere aft in the run. A steady stream of water could be seen running down alongside the keelson but it could not be traced to its source.

At about 3 p.m., the vessel's situation being now desperate, Captain Walters decided to run back for harbour. As the schooner bore away before wind and sea, a vessel was seen almost dead ahead and very close. For a few tense moments those on deck wondered whether the schooner would go clear, but she slid by with about 30 yards to spare. The stranger proved to be a tunnyman hove-to on the port tack under balance reefed mainsail and spitfire jib.

The wind had by now veered to W. by N. and moderated somewhat, but the sea was enormous.

When daylight came, the ship looked like a wreck. The hands were turned-to fishing the foreboom. This was completed by mid-day and the sail reset.

After running all day before a mountainous sea, the loom of the Bishop was picked up at 7.30 p.m. bearing about N.$\frac{1}{2}$ W., a very long way off, perhaps 25 to 30 miles ; and at 11 p.m. the loom of the Lizard was seen on the port beam. Course was now altered more to the nor'ard and at 11 o'clock the next morning *Bluenose* anchored in Plymouth Sound. The only luck she had on the trip was the strong fair wind that drove her home.

After docking at Plymouth for repairs, *Bluenose* set forth once more on her return passage across the Atlantic, arriving safely at Halifax after a comparatively uneventful crossing.

Her fishing career was now over and she spent her remaining years trading in the West Indies. A brief despatch in the spring of this year reported her loss on the coast of Haiti. Her passing closed another chapter in the long history of sail.

"WE SHOULD HAVE HAD THE POISSON"

By E. S. HARSTON

I DON'T think this story is altogether true, so that if any of the deleterious types who formed part of *Amokura*'s crew happen to read it, they shouldn't be misled. It deals with some of the yacht's wanderings during 1946, and to be logical should no doubt begin with a description of the yacht herself.

She was built in 1939 after a lot of thought. After all if we were going to have a war, there was no sense in building a yacht. On the other hand, if we were going to build a yacht there was no sense in having a war. So we built the boat : a 38-foot water-line bermuda yawl, designed by Fred Shepherd and built by Moodys ; the requirements being a sea-kindly family cruiser that would be fun to sail at weekends. She certainly came up both to expectations and specifications. Arthur Ransome has said that there is nothing so painful as building a yacht—or words to that effect. How right he is only those who roll romantic eyes and say inane things about dream ships don't know. But the pangs of parturition were worth it. She is a beauty, as a couple of races round the tins and a slashing cruise to the Scillies and Brest soon proved after her launching in 1939. (A picture of *Amokura* appears on **page 41**. Ed.).

When 1946 came, we took the yacht out of her mud berth and our creaking joints out of their shore going clothes. Roger Pinckney, who is not only vice-commodore of the R.C.C., but also cruises, had said he was going to St. Peter Port for Easter ; so, instead of following our own inclinations and going to Beaulieu, or even Yarmouth, we shipped a crew consisting of Ruth as cookie, Joe, Tompy and Jim and slid down the Hamble, round the Wight with the east going tide, and out into a disturbed stretch of water called the English Channel, where we promptly began to feel somewhat odd owing to the quartering sea.

As Joe said to Tompy during the graveyard watch : "Beating back against this sea won't be funny."

And Tompy replied to Joe, about half an hour later : "No."

That comprised the badinage of the watch, because I was listening in my little bunk below.

When I handed over at the end of my own watch some hours later, Tompy came on deck with the sweetest of smiles and said : "Skipper, I have just had puppies."

"What a happy thought," said I, "so will I." And did.

The joys of yachting !

However, we duly rounded the Casquets and slid down the Little Russel into St. Peter Port, tied up alongside a motor fishing vessel, and breathed more freely. Our first cruise, our first holiday, our first "foreign" port for six years. I had to pinch myself and say : "Relax you ass, this is really a holiday, the 'phone won't go, you have no appointments, nothing but the clear blue sea, the friendly folk of Guernsey, and drab old England of no beer, no spirits, no service, no anything is miles and miles behind you."

Roger arrived in *Dyarchy* and with his usual superb nonchalance blew in before the wind carrying everything, chose an anchorage, discarded it, chose another, dropped his hook and lowered away. A small 8-tonner piloted by a ruffian in a woollen hat turned out to be Humphrey Barton in *Dalua*. The Tews and Commander Graham were already there in *Mary Helen*. *White Pearl* owned by the Kendricks was there too. A Guernseyman told me that his son had rushed into his room exclaiming : "Daddy, daddy, they're back !"

"Who are back ?"

"The yachts—come and look !"

The yachts were there, but not on show, no gleaming brass, no glossy paint or varnish, just the barest "fit-out," but they had broken the ice.

This is hardly the place to talk of the Channel Islands and the war. All one can say is that although much had changed, the old welcoming friendliness was there as before. Everyone was busy painting, cleaning, repairing and removing the traces of the occupation. The old abounding supplies no longer existed, but the hospitable friendliness always shown to yachtsmen by Bucktrouts and everyone else was there as before.

We slipped off quietly in a gentle breeze and made for Sark. We lay with *Dyarchy* in the Havre Gosselin where the blue of the sea was beyond belief. We climbed the cliffs, our lungs filled with the gorgeous air. Joe took us to see the Dame of Sark and her husband back from his internment in Germany. Their stories would make a book. We grubby Londoners felt ourselves slowly reviving in their beautiful home.

At dusk we passed through the narrow channel between Brechou and Sark, went up the Great Russell, through the race and home to the Solent, determined to do it again at Whitsun—which is where the *poisson* comes in.

Now when Whitsun arrived the owner was somewhat sore stricken with divers diseases and the cruise began to look dim. The same crew plus Jeremy were assembled full of expectations. A gale had just blown itself out. No one hoping to enjoy himself would set sail across the Channel. So we decided to motor to Cowes and stay the night, which of course meant that we soon substituted Yarmouth for Cowes and ended in the Channel, bucketing about in the dark with the idea of getting to St. Peter Port after all. But the wind decided otherwise, and after pitching up and down in the same hole in the water for a very long time, we put on the engine gently and wandered across, picking up La Hague in the early morning where it was expected.

Sailing is productive of many theories ; the metacentric shelf, tacking to leeward, and so on, but the best of them all is Joe's theory that it is all done by springs and mirrors. It has never failed us. When the land appeared where it ought to be, he assured us that that was how it had been done, and we believed him.

The tide, however, was busy going up Channel, so we did some gentle thinking. It was no use bucking it for six hours, so why not go to Cherbourg for lunch ? or better still what about Omondville ? Omondville la Rogue ; romance, *vin blanc* and big *langouste ?* So Omondville it was, with magnifying glasses on the chart to distinguish the tiny harbour, and great expectations of lunch ashore in "furrin" parts.

We dropped the hook under the cumulative advice of the local fishermen. We hailed an ancient of days on the breakwater. Could we eat ashore ? Or should we practise *la cuisine Anglaise* and open a tin ? Assuredly we could eat ashore, *en ville.* So all those with beards stroked them, while the rest waxed their moustaches.

We boarded the dinghy and headed for the breakwater. The ancient of days told us that we could land by the buvette. Exquisite tact ! We landed there, it was his. Could we lunch—no *en ville*. *Un aperitif*—why certainly. But which ? With such exotic names it was hard to choose. But the remedy was simple. A row of glasses carried a sample of each. The skipper, ex-officio, drank them all and chose. The ancient approved. Would he join us and would Madame ? Why yes—but he disappeared round to the back of the buvette, only to reappear with a posy of flowers for Ruth. Some fishermen came in. Would they join us ? Much anxiety on the part of M'sieu and M'dame—they were only fishermen ! But they did and a good time was had by all. And so to the restaurant *en ville*.

"I know what will happen," said Jeremy, "no vin, no din, no nothing." And he was nearly right ; but, as the smiling owner assured us, Madame was on her way back from Cherbourg and all would be well. Madame arrived, chic, spotless. Lunch ? Why certainly, and on went a huge apron and in she went among the copper pots at two in the afternoon. *Langoustes* arrived with salad and *vin blanc* and suffered a merited fate. Our English tummies were replete, but the waiter arrived :

"Should they cook the *poisson* now ? "

We said we could not manage the *poisson*, but the waiter said there was steak to come after that ! Steak ? Yes, certainly. Well, we said we would have the steak, but couldn't manage the *poisson*. And so it was—acres of steak. We divided it in two and struggled to eat a half, and nearly succeeded, and sat back for the coffee. But weren't we going to eat the cheese ? Sorry, no cheese. Camembert ? Well—in that case, yes. And three Camemberts arrived. We ate one, and asked for the coffee. But there is a sweet ; Madame has made a sweet. So of course our better judgment gave way to our good intentions and a huge bowl of whipped cream and liqueur with strawberries went most decidedly west, chased by the coffee and *armagnac*.

And then Rene Clair took charge, or rather matters looked like one of his films. The crew, the proprietor, his friends—all of us processed through the village. The harbour master told us about the tides. The village came with us to the buvette. A couple of car loads from Cherbourg joined the crowd. Someone produced a pannikin and a bottle of cognac. Others asked whether they might dare to offer a drink to any of the crew ! If they had only known ! "Le Philips" appeared—a loud speaker geared to a gramophone and would we dance on the beach ? A cheerful soul struck up "God Save the King." The ship's company, not to be outdone la la-ed the "Marseillaise." A neat blonde model was detached from the outfit by her husband who explained that she was the mother of eight and from Paris.

The dinghy went slowly out to the yacht full of folk breathing stertorously and wondering in their comatose way when, if ever, they had eaten so much. Their dumbfounded tums were wondering the same. The sails went up and the yacht sailed slowly out beyond the breakwater for the Alderney race. The crowd still waved. So did we.

Joe looked very grave and thoughtful. Something obviously was on his mind. And at last it came out.

"Ernest," he said, "we should have had the *poisson*."

NEW YACHTS OF THE YEAR

O N the following sixty-two pages will be found the plans of a representative selection of the new yachts which have been completed or were under construction during 1946. They include sailing yachts, power craft, small boats and dinghies, and bearing in mind the great difficulties under which they had to work, both designers and builders are to be congratulated on the large number of new craft which have been launched throughout the year.

Early in the Spring, at a time when the boat-building industry was trying to turn over from war-time production to a peace-time economy, the ill-advised Government decided to impose a purchase tax on new sailing yachts; the tax was to be retrospective and to take effect as from February 20. No official announcement was ever made, though some vague information did leak out through the Customs authorities. It appeared that a sailing yacht was to be regarded as a toy or sports requisite, but power yachts were still to be classed as merchant vessels for they were to be exempted from the tax. As most sailing yachts have engines, and many power yachts carry sails, no one knew where the dividing line lay, and all requests for information were ignored.

Faced without warning by a sudden increase in price of $33\frac{1}{3}$ per cent, many would-be owners had to cancel their orders for new yachts, and others held them in abeyance until such time as a definite ruling from an authoritative source could be obtained. In the meantime those yards which were unable to employ their men on repairs or fitting out, continued to pay them, not knowing whether they would be able to give them work or not, and in this respect some of the smaller firms were very severely hit.

So the months passed in uncertainty, and not until June 25 did the Chancellor of the Exchequer make a statement in the House of Commons to the effect that he would remit the purchase tax on sailing yachts—a tax which, in fact, had never existed, and building operations were resumed.

Though one or two firms in pre-war years built yachts to a standard design, "stock" cruising yachts were not then popular; the average sailing man had a dread of entering a harbour and finding there one or more exact sister ships to his own; houses and motor cars might be standardized, but he still looked for individuality among boats. That view, however, seems to be changing. Nearly every new design is now called a "prototype," and most firms are standardizing on a particular design or series of designs, and are making plans to build more than just the one. This is logical in that when a naval architect has produced what he considers to be a perfect set of lines, there is no reason why he should be able to improve on them immediately. From the builder's point of view the stock boat saves a lot of trouble: the same set of moulds can be used for any number of boats, materials and fittings can be ordered in greater quantities, and considerable labour is saved. These things enable standard boats to be built more cheaply than individual boats, and the cheaper yachts become the more people will take to the sea for pleasure and recreation.

As many readers may wish to compare the accommodation of one design with that of another or perhaps work their own ideas on internal arrangements into a hull the lines of which please them, a scale of feet has been included with each drawing. In some cases the first foot of the scale has been divided into half or quarter feet.

" PEEKY "

A " Channel Class " Cutter

Designer	.	Laurent Giles & Partners, Ltd.
Builder.	.	Woodnutt and Co., Ltd., St. Helens, I.O.W.
Owner .	.	Cyril Davis.
L.O.A..	.	37 *ft.* 10½ *in.*
L.W.L..	.	26 *ft.*
Beam .	.	8 ft. 9 *in.*
Draught	.	6 *ft.*
Displacement	.	6.985 *tons.*
Sail area :		
Mainsail	.	340 *sq. ft.*
Staysail	.	97 *sq. ft.*
Jib (*No.* 1)		150 *sq. ft.*
Jib (*No.* 2)		89 *sq. ft.*
Yankee	.	286 *sq. ft.*
Genoa	.	411 *sq. ft.*

THIS 10-tonner is a direct descendant of the same designers' well-known *English Lass* and *Triune of Troy*, and they intend to establish this type as the " Channel Class," though not necessarily to a fixed set of lines.

Peeky was designed to provide the best possible combination of speed, seaworthiness and comfort on deck and below, and no attempt has been made to crowd too many berths into the available space, there being provision to sleep three only. Although this yacht will, no doubt, be entered for ocean racing events, the designers have not allowed themselves to be diverted from the above mentioned intentions by considerations of the R.O.R.C. rules.

Many people will be glad to see that the counter of this very pleasing design has been finished with a conventional raked transom instead of the vertical transom which this firm has almost established as a " trade-mark," and which has from time to time received some adverse criticism from the point of view of appearance. The two previous boats in the class carried no helm in any circumstances, and it is of interest to record that the designers, considering this to be an undesirable feature because of the difficulty of keeping such vessels on their course at sea, have altered the new design so that the yacht will carry a little weather helm.

The sail-plan shows a lofty rig, but with the staysail on a boom it should be easy to handle, while a varied combination of sails can be set to meet any and every condition.

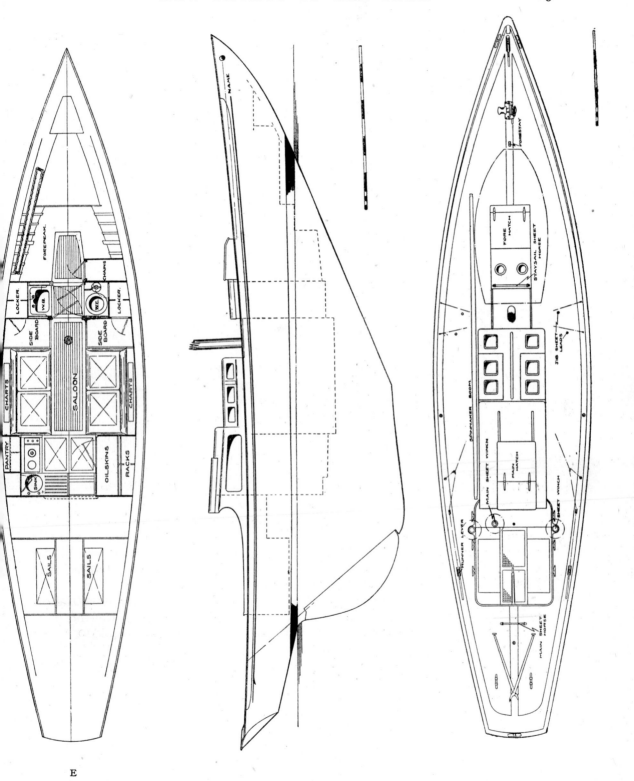

E

A 12-TON OFF-SHORE CRUISER

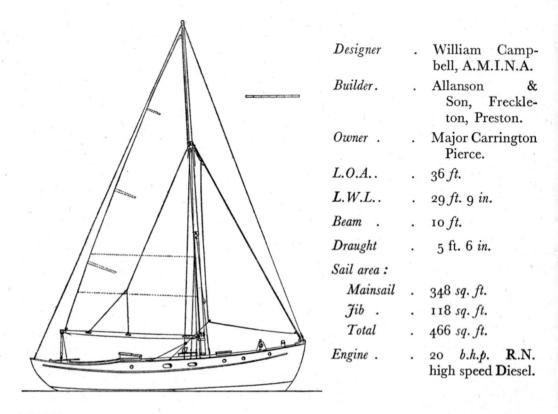

Designer	.	William Camp-bell, A.M.I.N.A.
Builder.	.	Allanson & Son, Freckle-ton, Preston.
Owner .	.	Major Carrington Pierce.
L.O.A..	.	36 *ft.*
L.W.L..	.	29 *ft.* 9 *in.*
Beam .	.	10 *ft.*
Draught	.	5 ft. 6 *in.*
Sail area :		
Mainsail	.	348 *sq. ft.*
Jib .	.	118 *sq. ft.*
Total	.	466 *sq. ft.*
Engine .	.	20 *b.h.p.* **R.N.** high speed **D**iesel.

THIS yacht was designed in 1939, but the war postponed her building until this year.

The owner required a vessel capable of standing up to heavy weather, with as much clear deck space as possible and six feet of headroom throughout. For these reasons built-up topsides and a flush deck take the place of the more usual cabin-top, and deadlights are fitted in the deck instead of a skylight, thereby eliminating leaks. The ample freeboard should help to keep the yacht dry at sea.

The rig, totalling 466 sq. ft., is a very snug one for a vessel of this type, and presumably good use will be made of the engine in light weather. As the owner did not wish to be bothered with runners, the mast has been given considerable rake and an extra shroud has been led well aft.

With a two-berth cabin for'ard, and saloon and galley combined, the accommodation is simply arranged and has plenty of floor space and excellent headroom.

A two-cylinder 20 b.h.p. R.N. high-speed Diesel engine is installed on the centre line with its controls grouped at the forward end of the self-draining cockpit.

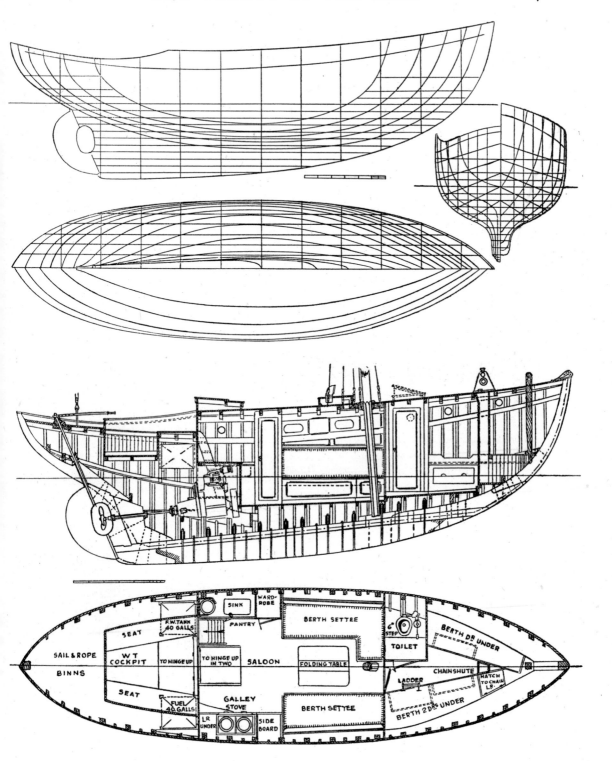

THE R.N.S.A. SOLANI CLASS

Designer	.	Maurice Griffiths
		G.M., A.I.N.A.
L.O.A.	.	38 ft. 8 in.
L.W.L..	.	28 ft. 5 in.
Beam .	.	10 ft. 6 in.
Draught	.	4 ft.
Draught with C.B..	.	6 ft. 5 in.
Lead keel	.	3.12 tons.
Displacement	.	7.38 tons.
Sail Area :		
Sloop .	.	645 sq. ft.
Ketch	.	720 sq. ft.

BEFORE the war had ended, the Royal Naval Sailing Association decided to obtain two designs for yachts which might appeal to their members, the Service Yacht Clubs, and possibly the Admiralty for the training of cadets. The smaller of these designs, *Meridian*, by Kenneth M. Gibbs, appears on page 70.

The larger design was to be equally suitable for deep water passage-making, coastal cruising, or ditch crawling. She must have comfortable accommodation for four people, or five at a pinch, be of moderate displacement and safe for an inexperienced crew. As the design was to be of the shoal draft centre-board type, Maurice Griffiths, who has had great experience in designing and sailing such craft, was asked to prepare the design. He produced a set of lines with easy flowing curves from bow to stern and with no reverse curve to the garboards, so that the planking could be done with the minimum wastage of timber, or metal or moulded ply could be used if desired. But after much consideration, the orthodox method of construction was decided on. The raised midship deck was adopted because it is stronger, cheaper, and less likely to leak than is the usual form of cabin-top, and in this instance it gives 5 ft. 10 in. headroom.

When the design had been completed it was shown to many leading yachtsmen in this and other countries and received their unqualified approval. But to prove that this vessel would be a good one, a 12 ft. 10 in. wax model was made and tried out most thoroughly in a 900 ft. testing tank. Under all conditions the model proved to be docile, carrying only a comfortable amount of weather helm, was easily controlled and had a comparatively high turn of speed.

One of these yachts has been built in India for deep sea fishing off the Seychelles Islands, and six are understood to be on order in this country. Two British yards are prepared to jig the design, and the estimated cost per ship, with a 10/20 h.p. engine, is £1,955.

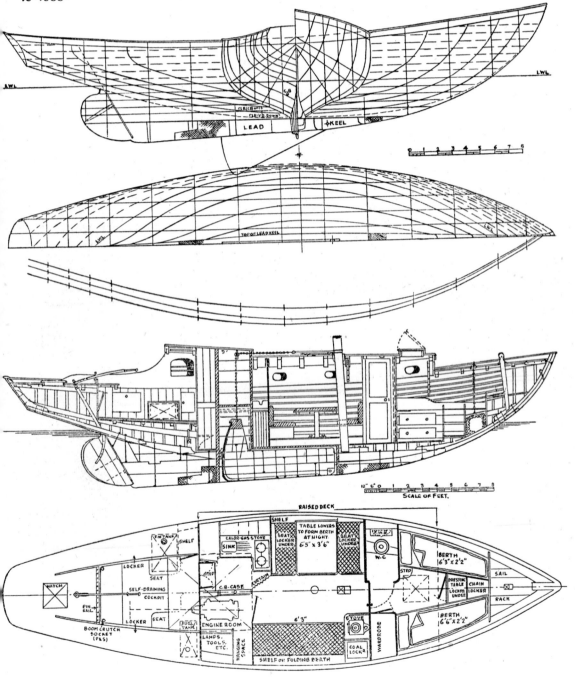

THE R.N.S.A. MERIDIAN CLASS

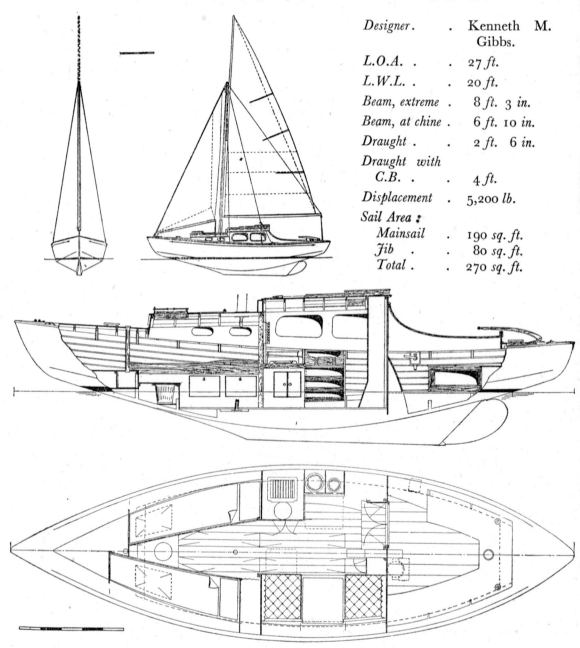

Designer.	.	Kenneth M. Gibbs.
L.O.A.	.	27 ft.
L.W.L.	.	20 ft.
Beam, extreme	.	8 ft. 3 in.
Beam, at chine	.	6 ft. 10 in.
Draught	.	2 ft. 6 in.
Draught with C.B.	.	4 ft.
Displacement	.	5,200 lb.
Sail Area :		
Mainsail	.	190 sq. ft.
Jib	.	80 sq. ft.
Total	.	270 sq. ft.

THE plans reproduced on this and the opposite page were originally drawn for a designing competition sponsored by *The Yachtsman* in 1944, for a 20-foot waterline centreboard cruiser suitable for week-ending, up river sailing and coastwise cruising

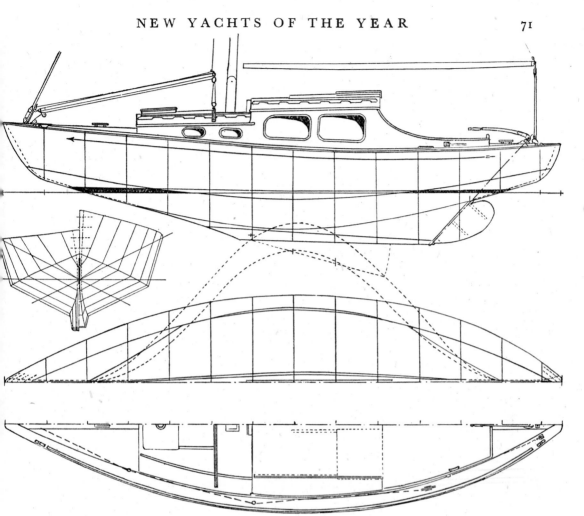

in summer weather. The judges of the competition, Mr. P. C. Crossley and the late T. Harrison Butler, awarded first prize to this design out of a total of 31 entries, and they commended it very highly. They stated in their report that this was the best chine bilge design they had ever seen, and that it was perfectly balanced, a condition rarely achieved in this type of hull.

Before the war had ended, the Royal Naval Sailing Association decided to obtain two designs for yachts which might appeal to their members, the Service Yacht Clubs, and perhaps to the Admiralty for the training of cadets. The larger of these designs, the *Solani* class by Maurice Griffiths, appears on page 68. For the smaller yacht Kenneth M. Gibbs's *Meridian* was chosen.

Certain modifications were made to the design. The dog-house was dispensed with, and bermuda rig replaced the sliding gunter, which in the original design had been arranged with a tabernacle so that the yacht might pass under bridges.

Two of this class have been built by The Lymington Shipyard. The first to be launched was *Firedrake* for Vice Admiral Sir Geoffrey Blake, K.C.B., D.S.O. A picture of this yacht appears on page 42.

A 35-FOOT FAMILY CRUISER

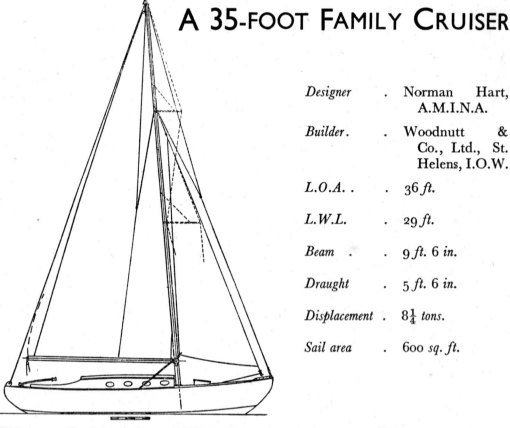

Designer	.	Norman Hart, A.M.I.N.A.
Builder.	.	Woodnutt & Co., Ltd., St. Helens, I.O.W.
L.O.A. .	.	36 ft.
L.W.L.	.	29 ft.
Beam .	.	9 ft. 6 in.
Draught	.	5 ft. 6 in.
Displacement	.	8¼ tons.
Sail area	.	600 sq. ft.

IN the words of the designer " This hull is like *Lady Mine* and *Mingulay*, and is the best sailing hull I know how to design."

A comfortable family cruiser was asked for, and this she should prove to be with her wide floor space in the cabin, her coal stove and partly sheltered cockpit. The galley with its hinged panel to fold down over the two burner cooking stove and sink when these are not in use, is unusual but practical, and 50 gallons of fresh water is a generous supply for a yacht of this size.

An interesting feature of the construction is that the frames are to be dovetailed into the deck beams, an arrangement which should give added strength when executed by a first-class shipwright.

As opening portholes in cabin-top coamings nearly always leak, the designer has cleverly arranged for them to leak on to something that does not matter. The large scale drawing (top right on the opposite page) shows the arrangement. A solid hand-rail is fastened to each coaming for its full length beneath the opening ports. These collect all the drips, and at their lowest points ⅜ inch pipes conduct the water neatly to the bilge.

The power unit has not yet been decided on, but this will probably be either a 2 cylinder Stuart Turner with reduction gear, or a Grey " Seascout," either of which should give the yacht a speed of 5–5½ knots.

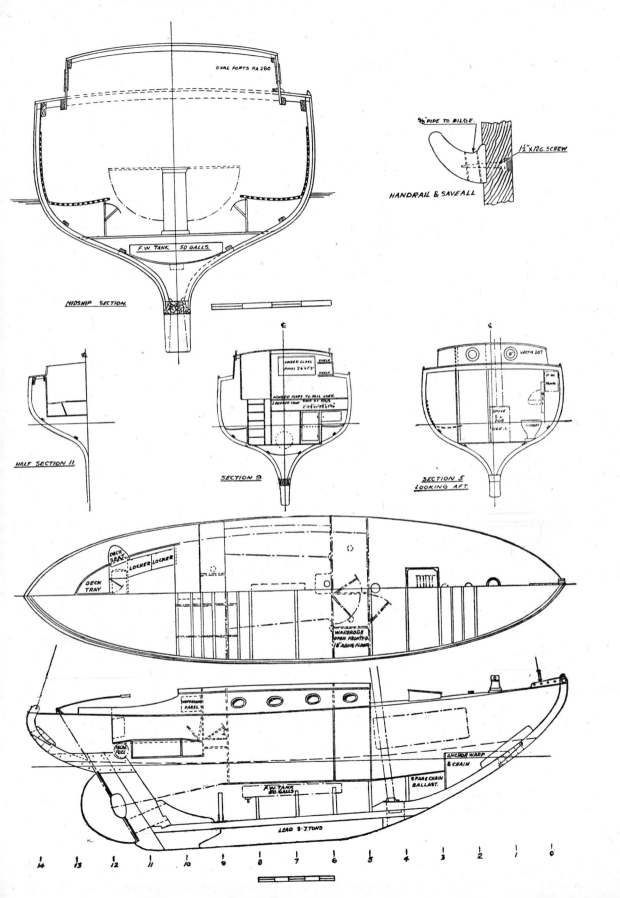

OVAL PORTS P.A. 280

F.W. TANK. 50 GALLS.

MIDSHIP SECTION.

⅜" PIPE TO BILGE.

1½"×12G. SCREW

HANDRAIL & SAVEALL

HALF SECTION II.

HINGED GLASS
PANEL 2'6"×1'3"

SHELF
SHELF

HINGED FLAPS TO FALL OVER.
2 BURNER STOVE

SECTION 9

VECTIS 287

STOVE
S.A.
208

VICTORY

SECTION 5
LOOKING AFT.

DECK
SEAT

LOCKER LOCKER

DECK
TRAY

WARDROBE
OPEN FRONTED.
18" ABOVE FLOOR.

IRON
FUEL

ANCHOR WARP
& CHAIN

F.W. TANK
50 GALLS.

SPARE CHAIN
BALLAST.

LEAD 3.7 TONS.

14   13   12   11   10   9   8   7   6   5   4   3   2   1   0

NESÆA

A 21-ton Bermuda Cutter

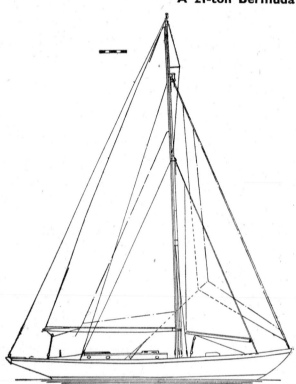

Designer .	.	C. E. Nicholson.
Builder .	.	Camper & Nicholsons, Ltd., Gosport.
Owner .	.	C. E. A. Hartridge.
L.O.A. .	.	51 *ft.* 7 *in.*
L.W.L. .	.	37 *ft.*
Beam .	.	11 *ft.* 2 *in.*
Draught .	.	7 *ft.* 7 *in.*
Engine .	.	4 *cyl.* Gray.

NO collection of yacht designs could be representative without including something from the board of Mr. C. E. Nicholson, so although at the time of going to press the firm of Camper & Nicholsons have not built any post-war yachts, we are publishing the plans of two of their vessels which have proved to be popular and of which more will be built as soon as conditions improve.

Nesæa whose plans appear here was laid down as a " stock " boat, as is often the case with yards that find themselves short of work during the summer. She was designed purely as a fast cruising yacht and with no intention of more than an occasional handicap race, but it is felt that she would perform well under R.O.R.C. rating. The lay-out below is comparatively orthodox, but the propeller installation is of particular interest, and was first adopted by the firm in the case of the ketch *Gwendolen*; it is considered to be one of the most efficient methods of auxiliary propulsion. The shaft is slightly offset on the side of the rudder post, and a casting attached to the fin above the rudder brings the propeller to perfectly clear water. The engine is a Gray and is fitted with reduction gear.

Camper & Nicholsons hope shortly to build a number of yachts a little smaller than *Nesæa*, and the accommodation will embody requirements for the " owner-skipper ; " space for a paid hand will only be provided if specially desired.

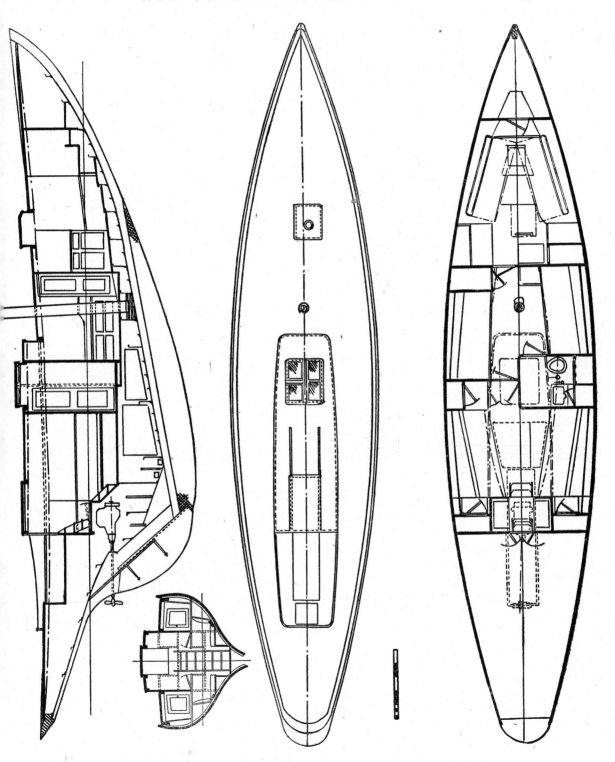

SALUKI

A new "Long Gauntlet"

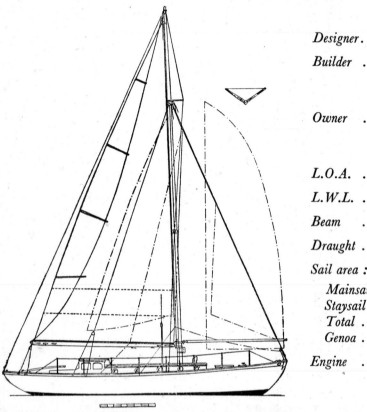

Designer.	.	H. G. May.
Builder .	.	The Berthon Boat Co., Ltd., Lymington.
Owner .	.	Major W. M. Martineau, M.C.
L.O.A. .	.	41 ft.
L.W.L. .	.	33 ft.
Beam .	.	9 ft. 8 in.
Draught .	.	5 ft. 10½ in.
Sail area :		
Mainsail	.	461 sq. ft.
Staysail	.	211 sq. ft.
Total .	.	672 sq. ft.
Genoa .	.	330 sq. ft.
Engine .	.	12 h.p. Parsons petrol engine.

THE lines of this new yacht are the same as those of *Lollypoppet*, a 14-tonner designed by Mr. H. G. May for his own use and built in 1939. She won the Cross Channel race in that year.

Saluki's accommodation, however, is quite different and has been arranged to suit the requirements of her owner. With a double berth cabin for'ard, and two settee berths in the saloon, there is comfortable accommodation for four, the bedding for the saloon berths being stowed behind the settee backs. Two very comfortable seats are arranged each side in the deckhouse-companionway, and the galley at the aft end of the saloon has penty of space. At present a Para-Fin stove is installed there, but this is to be replaced by a Calor Gas cooker.

On deck everything is as simple as possible. The runners are set up by Highfield levers, winches take the headsail sheets, and a most ingenious winch supplied by F. W. Bracket & Co., of Colchester, clamped to the mast, deals with the halyards.

A Parsons petrol engine developing 12 b.h.p. at 1,000–1,100 r.p.m. has plenty of space to itself beneath the cockpit and companion steps.

A photograph of the yacht appears on page 42.

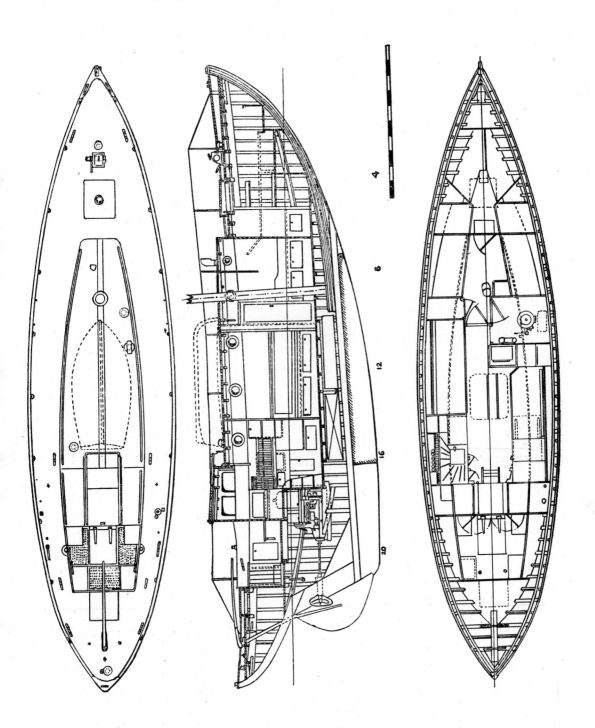

PETER DUCK

Designer .	.	Laurent Giles & Partners
Owner .	.	Arthur Ransome.
Builder .	.	Harry King & Son, Pinmill.
L.O.A. .	.	28 *ft.* 3 *in.*
L.W.L. .	.	25 *ft.*
Beam .	.	9 *ft.*
Draught .	.	3 *ft.* 6 *in.*
Displacement	.	5.61 *tons.*
Sail Area :		
Mainsail .	.	160 *sq. ft.*
Staysail .	.	66 *sq. ft.*
Mizzen .	.	67 *sq. ft.*
Genoa .	.	178 *sq. ft.*
Engine .	.	8 *h.p.* Stuart Turner.

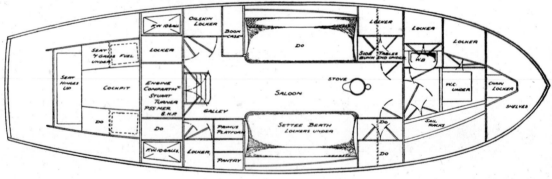

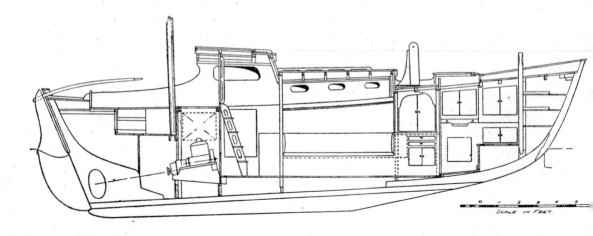

SCALE IN FEET.

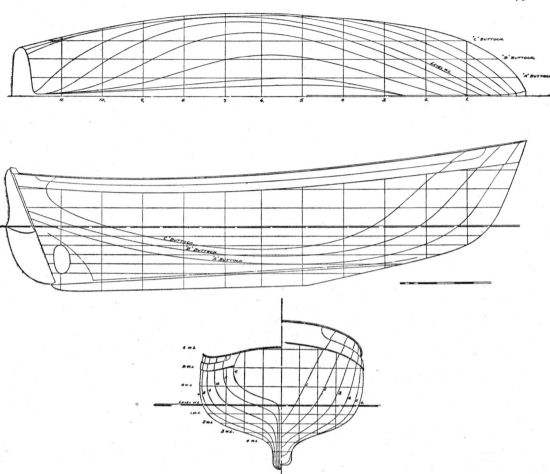

FOR a number of years the owner of *Peter Duck*, a well-known author, has been building little ships in which to work. The last was completed in 1939, but she was too large for single-handed sailing and strictly curtailed physical powers. So, having a virtually new ship for sale, the owner was able to instruct Harry King to go right ahead.

For the new boat Laurent Giles was asked to prepare designs. These were to provide the maximum of livability with the absolute minimum of work. Somehow drawings were got out in time for King to start work in January 1946. But it is an odd fact that rush jobs often turn out well and Giles, always happy with traditional types, has drawn a most attractive little ship. Those who have followed this designer's work will recognise *Peter Duck's* antecedents : *Argo, Wanderer II* and *Kalliste*. Beam is increased to compensate for shallow draught and the bow is placed in the manner of his motor cruisers of the *Samaki* type. Since designing *Wapipi*, Giles has specialised in shallow draught, and it is a fair bet that *Peter Duck* will be staunch and weatherly within the limits of her type. The ketch rig would not be everyone's choice, but there is no doubt that she carries the rig and sits on the water most attractively.

AN 8-TON AUXILIARY SLOOP

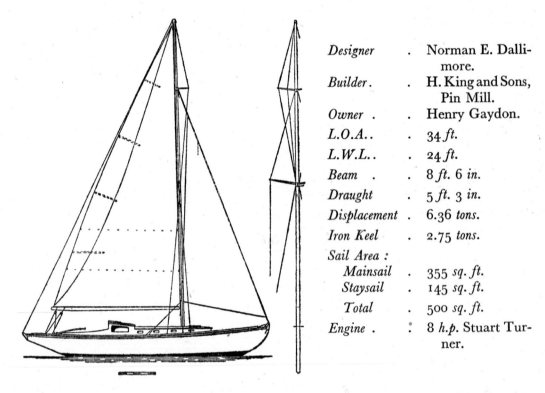

Designer	.	Norman E. Dalli-more.
Builder .	.	H. King and Sons, Pin Mill.
Owner .	.	Henry Gaydon.
L.O.A..	.	34 ft.
L.W.L..	.	24 ft.
Beam .	.	8 ft. 6 in.
Draught	.	5 ft. 3 in.
Displacement	.	6.36 tons.
Iron Keel	.	2.75 tons.
Sail Area :		
Mainsail	.	355 sq. ft.
Staysail	.	145 sq. ft.
Total	.	500 sq. ft.
Engine .	:	8 h.p. Stuart Tur-ner.

Having chartered the Dallimore designed cutter *Phynella* (11 tons), Mr. Gaydon was so impressed with her ease of handling and ample accommodation that he wished to have her reproduced for himself. But owing to the cost of building, it was decided to reduce the size to 8 tons, and yet retain as much of the accommodation as possible.

Such an endeavour is often the ruination of a design, but as the accompanying plans show, Mr. Dallimore has certainly succeeded without any ill effects in producing a comfortable little cruiser for the owner, his wife and two youngsters, and has managed to obtain 5 ft. 9 in. headroom without resorting to an abnormally high cabin-top.

An 8 h.p. Stuart Turner engine is to be installed beneath the dog-house floor to drive a centrally placed propeller, and should give the yacht a speed of 5–6 knots.

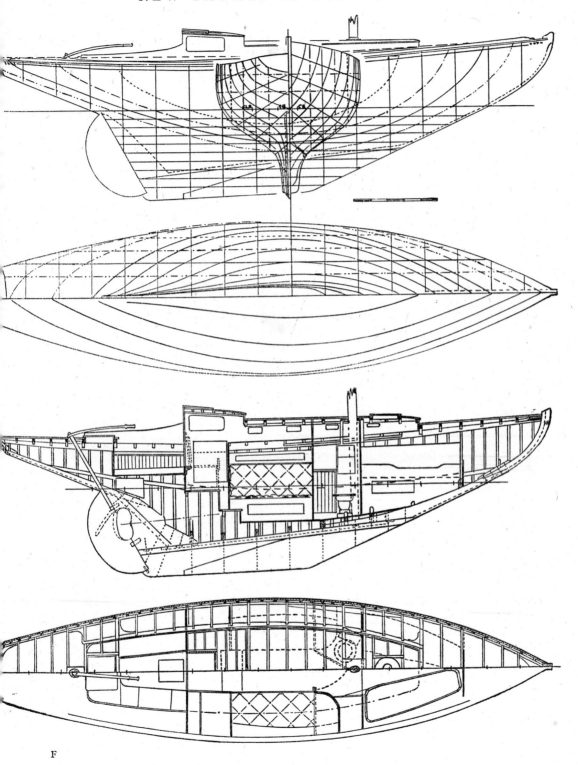

WEST OF ENGLAND ONE DESIGN CLASS

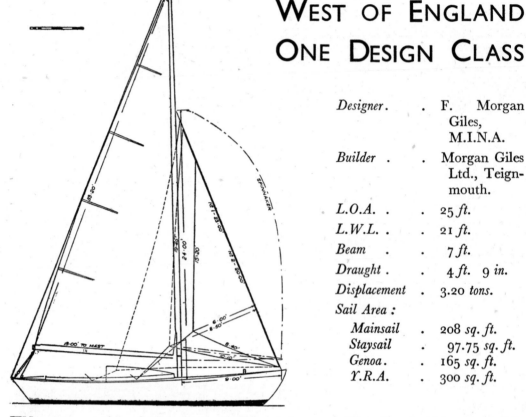

Designer.	.	F. Morgan Giles, M.I.N.A.
Builder	.	Morgan Giles Ltd., Teignmouth.
L.O.A.	.	25 *ft.*
L.W.L.	.	21 *ft.*
Beam	.	7 *ft.*
Draught.	.	4 *ft.* 9 *in.*
Displacement	.	3.20 *tons.*
Sail Area :		
Mainsail	.	208 *sq. ft.*
Staysail	.	97.75 *sq. ft.*
Genoa.	.	165 *sq. ft.*
Y.R.A.	.	300 *sq. ft.*

IN 1945 a meeting of 18 yacht and sailing clubs was held to discuss what steps might best be taken to revive yachting along the coast from Portland to Land's End, and it was decided to bring into being a one design class suitable for open sea racing at West Country ports and passage racing between those ports. A number of designers were invited to submit suggestions on a specification outlined by the Committee, and Mr. Morgan Giles' design was the one selected.

The designer was of the opinion that the obvious type of boat was an up-to-date edition of the Falmouth Quay Punt. The short overhang for'ard and the transom stern would simplify construction, and the ample draught would enable the displacement to be cut down and so make possible an easily driven boat capable of being sailed in broken water with the minimum of canvas.

The price was not to exceed £500 complete and ready for sea, and that this design met with general approval was soon evident, for early this year orders had been booked for six boats, and two more were to follow. The sudden imposition of the purchase tax, however, held up the whole project. It is unfortunate that in the meantime there have been further advances in the cost of labour and materials—especially in the price of lead ballast—which will make it impossible to keep to the original estimate. But with the repeal of the tax, several of the original prospective owners have shown a renewal of interest, and it is hoped that the class will come into being in 1947. Meanwhile the prototype boat is nearing completion.

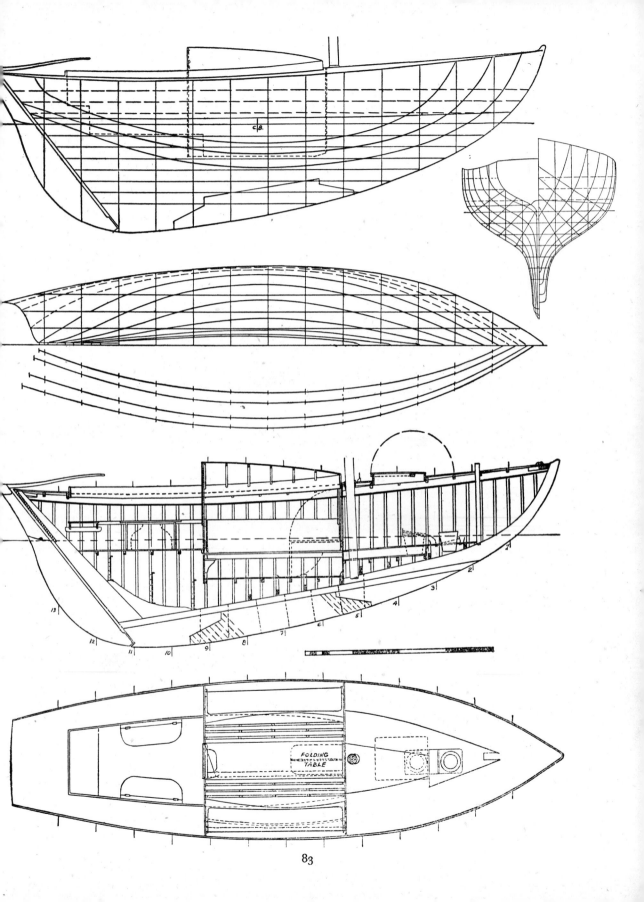

C.B.

FOLDING TABLE

FREEDOM

A 7½-ton Cruiser

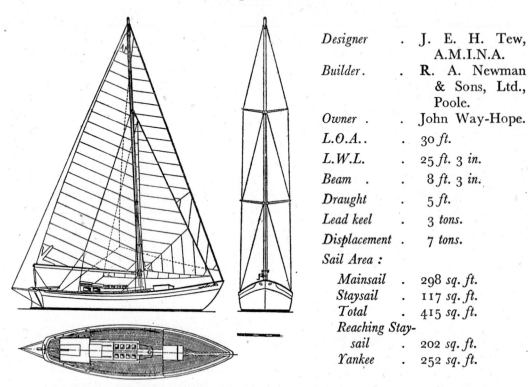

Designer	.	J. E. H. Tew, A.M.I.N.A.
Builder.	.	R. A. Newman & Sons, Ltd., Poole.
Owner .	.	John Way-Hope.
L.O.A..	.	30 *ft.*
L.W.L.	.	25 *ft.* 3 *in.*
Beam .	.	8 *ft.* 3 *in.*
Draught	.	5 *ft.*
Lead keel	.	3 *tons.*
Displacement .		7 *tons.*
Sail Area :		
Mainsail	.	298 *sq. ft.*
Staysail	.	117 *sq. ft.*
Total	.	415 *sq. ft.*
Reaching Stay-sail	.	202 *sq. ft.*
Yankee	.	252 *sq. ft.*

ALTHOUGH she has sleeping accommodation in real comfort for three and one in a pipe cot, *Freedom* was designed with the intention that she should be easily handled by one man ; with the headsails hanked to stays and Highfield levers used to work the runners, she certainly should be easy for a lone hand.

She was launched from the yard of R. A. Newman & Sons in August 1946, and has proved to be stiff, very handy and faster than expected. Her big, upswept bow with plenty of flare keeps her dry in a headsea, and provides a safe position for the pram dinghy upside down over the fore hatch.

John Tew had built-up topsides in way of the cabin in *Mary Helen*, the first yacht he designed. That arrangement proved to be a great success in every way, eliminating deck leaks and providing a real air of spaciousness below. So it was only to be expected that *Freedom* would have built-up topsides as well. But with the forehatch joined to the for'ard coaming of the raised deck, there would be some risk of water lodging against it on the weather side. In building, therefore, the hatch has been moved one beam further for'ard so as to leave a draining space between it and the raised deck.

The yacht has been fitted with an engine, but as this is still in the experimental stage, nothing can be said about it yet.

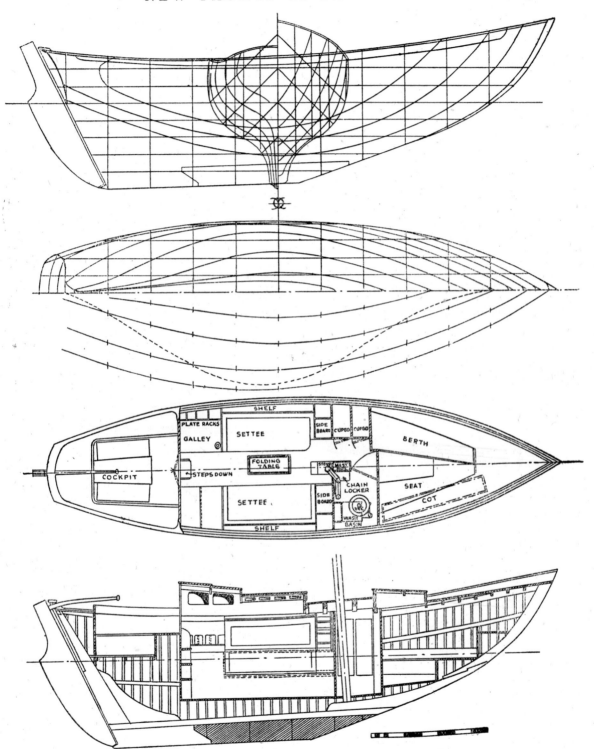

MARY AIDAN

7-ton Auxiliary Sloop

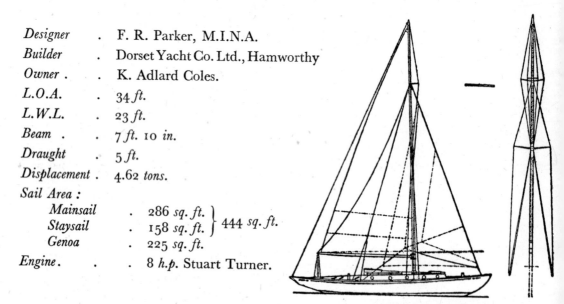

Designer	.	F. R. Parker, M.I.N.A.
Builder	.	Dorset Yacht Co. Ltd., Hamworthy
Owner .	.	K. Adlard Coles.
L.O.A.	.	34 ft.
L.W.L.	.	23 ft.
Beam .	.	7 ft. 10 in.
Draught	.	5 ft.
Displacement .		4.62 tons.

Sail Area :
Mainsail	.	286 sq. ft.	} 444 sq. ft.
Staysail	.	158 sq. ft.	
Genoa	.	225 sq. ft.	
Engine .	.	8 h.p. Stuart Turner.	

UNDER the name *Halcyon* this design won a second prize in a competition for a 23 ft. waterline fast cruiser sponsored by *The Yachtsman* in 1945. Early this year building was commenced by the Dorset Yacht Company at Hamworthy, Poole, and before the hull was planked Mr. K. Adlard Coles, editor of *The Yachtsman*, bought her and she was launched in June. A second yacht to this design known as The Dyco Halcyon Class, is now under construction.

With the cabin top carried through for'ard of the mast the boat has good headroom and plenty of light below. Though no engine is shown on the plans, *Mary Aidan* has been fitted with a 2 cylinder 8 h.p. Stuart Turner engine which gives her a speed of approximately 5 knots. The price complete but subject to specification is £2,250.

The self draining cockpit is a large one, well protected and comfortable to steer from. It is of interest to note that the tiller was arranged in the now fashionable internal position, but in practice this was found to be somewhat unsatisfactory as it could not be put hard over in an emergency, also it took up a good deal of valuable room. The builders, being anxious to get their prototype correct in every detail, have replaced it with a conventional tiller with the rudder head above deck.

A 6½ foot dinghy stowes neatly on the cabintop where it is well out of the way.

A picture of *Mary Aden* appears on page 46.

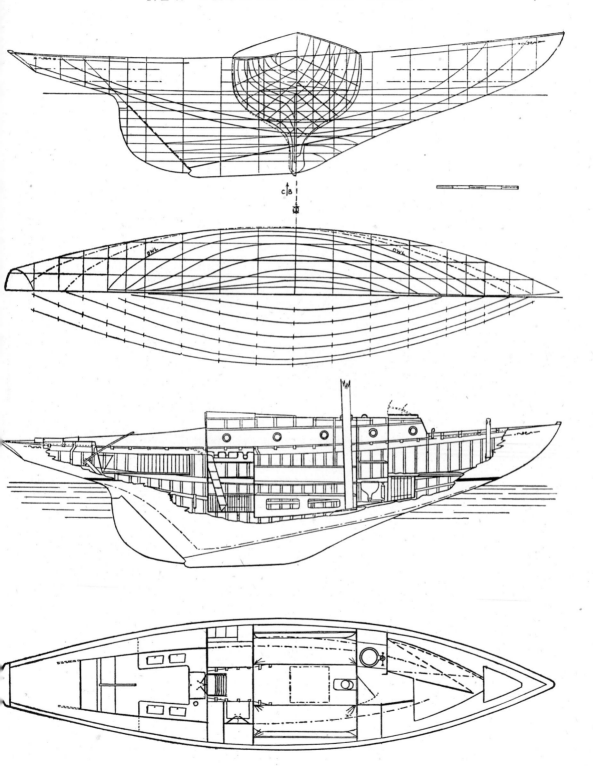

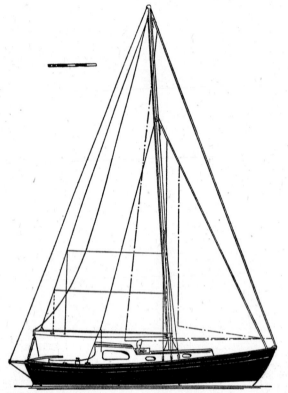

THE VERTUE
CLASS

Designer .	.	Laurent Giles and Partners.
L.O.A. .	.	25 *ft.* 3 *in.*
L.W.L. .	.	21 *ft.* 6 *in.*
Beam	.	7 *ft.* 2 *in.*
Draught .	.	4 *ft.* 6 *in.*
Displacement	.	4.213 *tons.*
Sail Area :		
Mainsail	.	201 *sq. ft.*
Staysail	.	93 *sq. ft.*
2nd Staysail .		67 *sq. ft.*
Genoa .	.	229 *sq. ft.*

THESE 5-tonners are the post-war version of *Monie*, built in 1938, and the leader of a fleet of about a dozen at the outbreak of war. They are named the Vertue Class in recognition of Col. Biddle's cruise to the Bay of Biscay and back in 1939, for which he was awarded the Little Ship Club Vertue Cup for the best cruise of the year. They have twice won R.C.C. awards for extended cruises.

The design has, therefore, been well tried, and these little ships have proved themselves such excellent cruising vessels that no alteration has been made to the hull form or sail-plan. Improvements in accommodation have, however, been made to give them increased space below decks.

This has been achieved by the addition of a small dog-house, by carrying the coachroof through to the fore hatch and by stepping the mast in a socket on deck. The result has been to obtain 6 feet headroom under the dog-house and uninterrupted passage through to the fo'c's'le with a minimum of 5 feet headroom under the extended coachroof. The fo'c's'le now becomes easy of access and provides an adequate cabin for a third person.

To carry the thrust of the mast, four pillars are arranged with deck stiffening over, the forward stiffeners forming part of the fo'c's'le bulkhead. This arrangement has proved to be successful in previous Giles designed boats.

Of the six Vertue Class boats now building, two have departed from the standard lay-out. One of these for Dr. K. E. Yuill, has a built-in berth to starboard and a 4-foot upholstered settee to port ; the other, for Mr. Peter Kinnersley, has an enlarged cockpit and two built-in berths on the starboard side. This boat is intended for fishing among the Channel Islands and cruising on the Brittany coast.

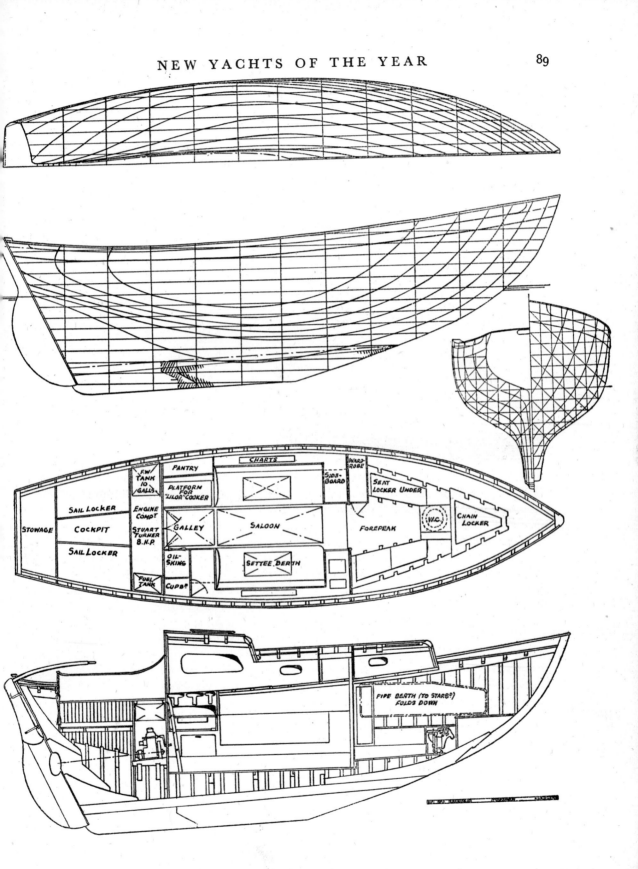

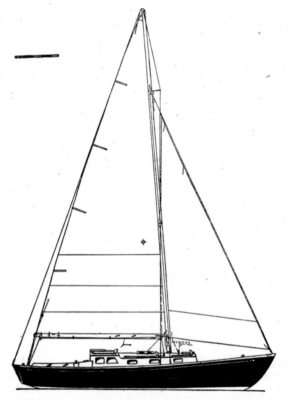

GEFARE

30-foot Auxiliary Sloop

Designer .	.	Arthur C. Robb.
Builder .	.	Gefare, Ltd., Ipswich.
L.O.A. .	.	30 ft. 3 in.
L.W.L. .	.	23 ft. 6 in.
Beam .	.	8 ft. 6 in.
Draught .	.	4 ft. 7 in.
Sail Area :		
Mainsail	.	275 sq. ft.
Staysail	.	150 sq. ft.
Total .	.	425 sq. ft.
Engine .	.	Morris Vedette.

THE sponsor of this design (who desires to be anonymous for the present) believes that a demand exists for the smallest possible auxiliary cruiser providing a separate sleeping cabin, galley, toilet and over 6 ft. headroom, combined with a smart appearance and good performance under sail and power.

The dimensions of the boat as designed appear to be the absolute minimum to meet these requirements, if the lines and appearance are not to be seriously influenced by the accommodation. The boat should perform quite well, and although no consideration whatever has been given to racing or the influence of any of the current rules, she might easily provide a most economical and interesting one-design class, or compete in some of the medium distance races with a prospect of success.

Construction will be to the highest yacht standard compatible with Government controls. The prototype boat now building will have grown oak frames and bent timbers, but whether the subsequent boats will have bonderised and galvanised steel frames and bent timbers, or all bent timbers, has not yet been decided. The most noticeable feature will be the mast stepped on the coachroof. Thorough attention has been given to ensuring that this will prove practicable, and an excess of strength has been provided, while the mast will be of slightly greater dimensions for the same wall thickness than usual. The advantage in planning the accommodation will be obvious.

The prototype is now building and immediately after completion and trials, Messrs. Gefare of Ipswich propose to lay down at least six of these boats for the 1947 season. Allowance has been made for several alternative makes and types of engine.

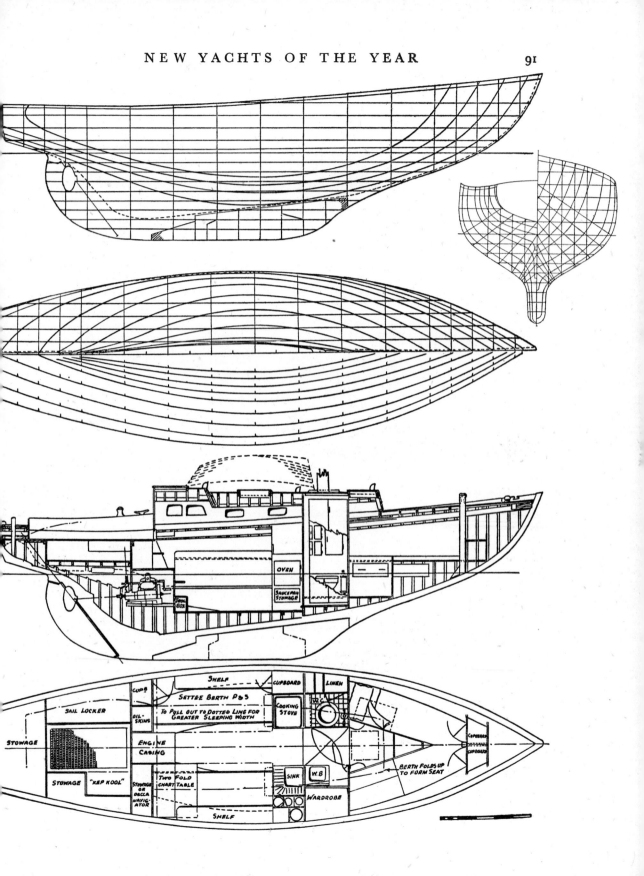

PUFFIN

A 4½-ton Cruiser

Designer	.	Harold H. Dawes, A.M.I.N.A.
Builder	.	Lady Bee Ltd., Shoreham.
Owner	.	Miss Dyson.
L.O.A.	.	24 ft. 6 in.
L.W.L.	.	19 ft.
Beam	.	7 ft. 1 in.
Draught	.	4 ft.
Iron keel	.	18 cwt.
Displacement	.	3 tons.
Sail Area :		
Mainsail	.	194 sq. ft.
Staysail	.	80 sq. ft.
Total	.	274 sq. ft.
Engine	.	8 h.p. Stuart Turner.

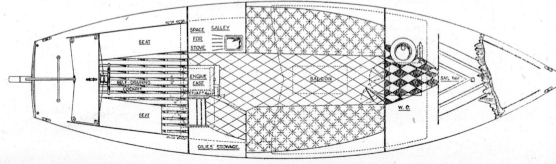

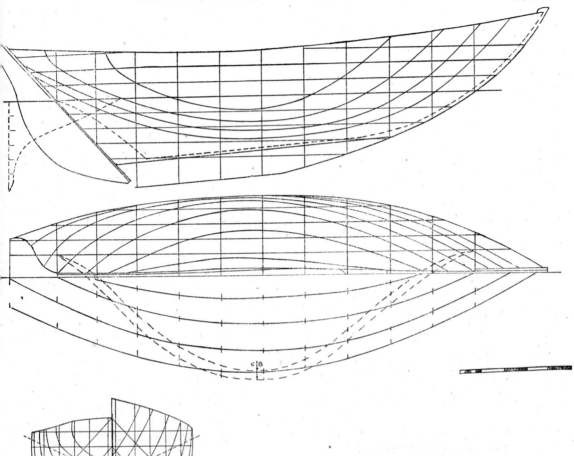

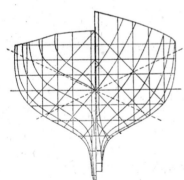

THE owner asked for a fast sailer with a pleasing profile and good manœuvreability, raised cabin-top over the galley—which will afford a measure of protection to the helmsman—water-tight cockpit and wheel steering. The accommodation was to be arranged to be lived in for long periods when required.

The sections suggest that the boat will be reasonably stiff; the bow and buttock lines have a fair run and flatten out aft, while the diagonals indicate that she will plank up easily. To give her an easier motion 9 cwts of ballast will be stowed inside.

A 4 h.p. Stuart Turner engine with reduction and reverse gear was originally specified to be installed under the for'ard end of the cockpit. This should give ample power for such a vessel, but the owner decided instead to have an 8 h.p. engine without reduction gear. The extra weight and cost of this is, in the designer's opinion, not likely to be justified.

A sister ship to *Puffin* has been laid down as a stock cruiser by the same firm. She will have the smaller engine and will be fitted with a tiller instead of wheel steering.

MYONA

A Fast Day Cruiser

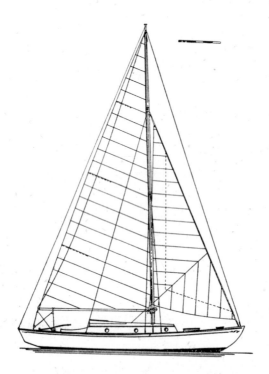

Designer	.	W. G. McBryde, M.I.N.A.
Builder.	.	Henry Rooke, East Cowes.
Owner .	.	N. B. Macbeth.
L.O.A..	.	27 *ft.*
L.W.L..	.	21 *ft.*
Beam .	.	7 *ft.*
Draught	.	4 *ft.*
Lead Keel	.	3,200 *lbs.*
Sail Area :		
Mainsail	.	218 *sq. ft.*
Staysail	.	105 *sq. ft.*
Total	.	323 *sq. ft.*
Engine .	.	Watermota 3 *b.h.p.*

ALTHOUGH Mr. N. B. Macbeth asked the designer to produce first and foremost a fast day cruiser, *Myona* possesses very useful cabin accommodation with a fine impression of roominess. The lay-out, with two settee berths, galley arranged aft, and w.c. and stowage for sails and gear for'ard, is simple and straightforward ; with the cabin-top carried forward of the mast—an innovation which is becoming more and more popular—there is good headroom throughout for a vessel of this size.

The simple inboard rig, totalling 323 sq. ft. is efficient and easy to handle under all conditions, and the anchor chain is dealt with by a mast winch.

The 3 b.h.p. single cylinder Watermota engine is installed very neatly beneath the companion steps where, although out of sight and not at all in the way, it is easily reached for inspection or adjustment when necessary.

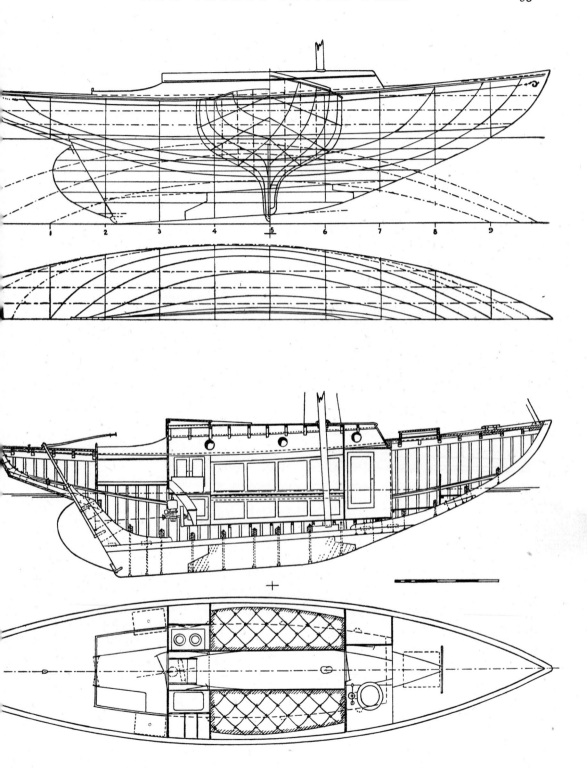

MARIMBA

A 4½-ton Estuary Cruiser

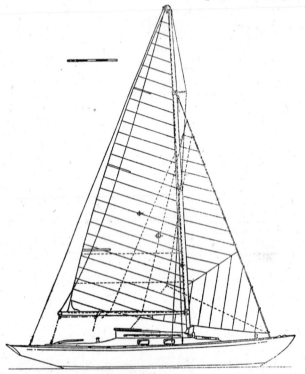

Designer .	.	John E. Powell
L.O.A. .	.	29 *ft.*
L.W.L. .	.	19 *ft.* 6 *in.*
Beam .	.	7 *ft.*
Draught .	.	4 *ft.* 3 *in.*
Displacement	.	2.9 *tons.*
Sail area .	.	310 *sq. ft.*

AN exact replica of this design 25 feet over all and proportionately scaled down in other respects, was laid down early this year at a yard in Dunlaoghaire, Eire. Lack of materials held up construction, but the yacht should be completed this year, together with a full-sized one. Considerable interest has been shown in the design in Ireland, and it is possible that six more will be built in 1947.

The design is for a fast but seaworthy light displacement estuary cruiser, having moderate overhangs, a simple rig and accommodation for two people. The lines show an easily driven hull with sections of sufficient power to carry a good spread of canvas, while the deadrise should allow reasonable comfort in a seaway. Enough straight has been given to the profile of the keel for ease in slipping.

Although the cabintop extends for'ard of the mast, it does not increase the headroom there, for orthodox main beams and partners have been fitted ; but the designer considered that the opportunity of having a compact system of built in water box ventilation ought not to be ignored. As space beneath the fore hatch was so restricted, the w.c. was placed aft, a position which is likely to receive some criticism.

It will be noticed that the sail-plan shows no runners. The designer explains that the pull of the headsail is resolved between the permanent backstay, main shrouds and a system of jumper struts and stays which should damp out the bending moments in all directions, be simple to construct and cheap to maintain. The working headsail has been cut with a high clew to allow good vision.

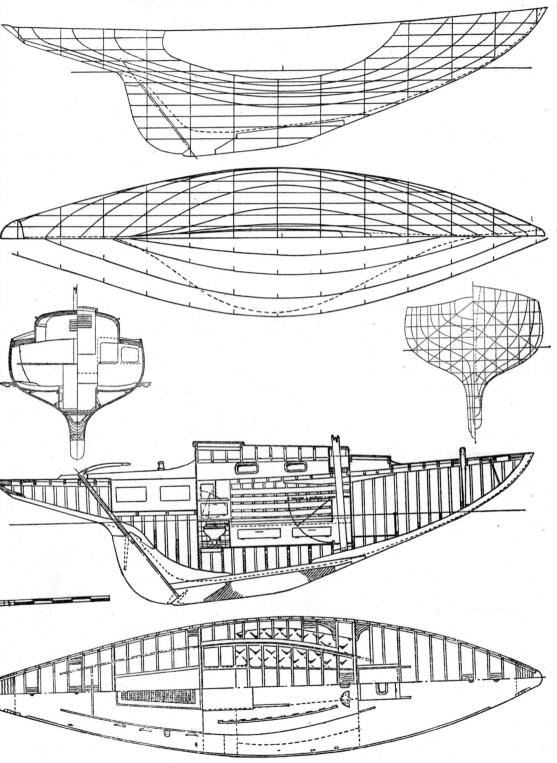

XYRIS

A 30-foot Auxiliary Sloop

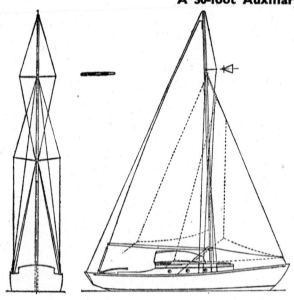

Designer.	.	C. E. Nicholson.
Builder .	.	Camper & Nicholsons, Ltd.,Gosport
Owner .	.	J. F. Lapthorn
L.O.A. .	.	30 *ft.*
L.W.L. .	.	23 *ft.*
Beam .	.	8 *ft.*
Draught .	.	4 *ft.* 5 *in.*
Sail Area	.	389 *sq. ft.*
Engine .	.	4 *cyl.* Morris Vedette.

THE *Xyris* class has proved to be one of the most popular of the Camper & Nicholsons' designs. Six of these boats were built in 1939, and although none have been built since the war, we think readers may be interested in their sail and accommodation plans. Basically the design was identical in all the boats with a view to economy in construction, but the internal arrangements all differed slightly according to the owners' requirements.

They were designed purely as handy knockabout cruisers and were built to a comprehensive specification and with a very complete inventory for £850, but it is of interest to note that *Xyris* won the Island Sailing Club's Jubilee race in 1939 against a large and varied fleet.

Although not built to Lloyds class, their construction plans were examined and they were given a term of 7 years Class B.

The sail-plan is very simple and, fitted as it is with jumper stays, the runners need only be set up when it is desired to have the leading edge of the staysail as straight as possible for racing.

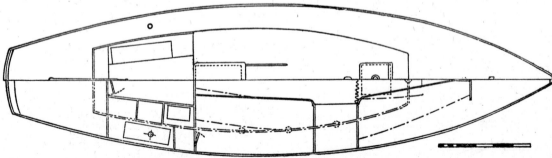

MIRTH

A Fast Day Cruiser

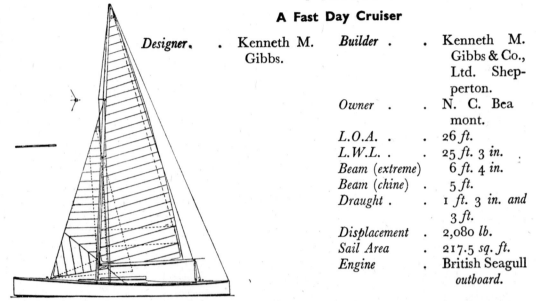

Designer.	. Kenneth M. Gibbs.	Builder .	. Kenneth M. Gibbs & Co., Ltd. Shepperton.
		Owner .	. N. C. Beamont.
		L.O.A. .	. 26 ft.
		L.W.L. .	. 25 ft. 3 in.
		Beam (extreme)	6 ft. 4 in.
		Beam (chine) .	5 ft.
		Draught .	. 1 ft. 3 in. and 3 ft.
		Displacement	. 2,080 lb.
		Sail Area .	. 217.5 sq. ft.
		Engine .	. British Seagull outboard.

MR. BEAUMONT required a fast centreboard boat chiefly for day sailing, but with sufficient cabin accommodation so that he and his son could camp out for a night or two, and to provide protection for cooking and meals in bad weather. Special emphasis was to be placed on speed, weatherliness and general handiness, in short the boat was to handle like a big racing dinghy but without the necessity for the crew to sit her up. The design was adopted from Mr. Gibbs' standard 15 sq. metre sharpie, and both he and the owner expected the boat to be somewhat wet. Instead, she proved to be unusually dry even in a short steep sea, and although she will turn in her own length, she is steady on the helm.

The cabintop is arranged to lift, and although it looks unsightly when raised, it works well and gives full sitting headroom.

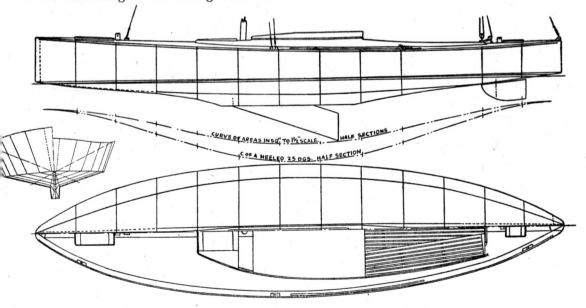

FIDALGA II

A 41-foot Motor Sailing Cruiser

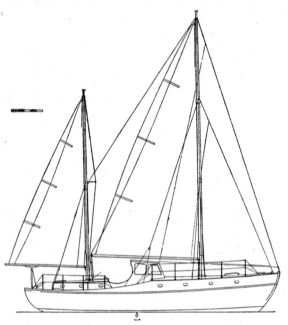

Designer .	.	John I. Thorny-croft and Co., Ltd.
Builder .	.	John I. Thorny-croft and Co., Ltd.
Owner .	.	K. C. Barnaby, O.B.E.
L.O.A. .	.	41 *ft.*
L.W.L. .	.	34 *ft.* 9 *in.*
Beam .	.	11 *ft.* 6 *in.*
Draught .	.	5 *ft.*
Thames Measure-ment .	.	18 *tons.*
Engine .	.	Thornycroft RTR/6 40 b.h.p. Diesel.
Speed under power .	.	8 *knots.*
Sail Area .	.	615 *sq. ft.*

JUST before the war, interest in the motor sailing cruiser type of yacht was increasing rapidly, and notable among the new designs was *Fidalga*, a 13-ton "fifty-fifty." Unlike many so-called motor sailers, her performance under sail and power was in every way successful. Her owner, Mr. K. C. Barnaby, was so pleased with her that he decided to have built a second *Fidalga* of similar design but with slightly larger dimensions. The building of this vessel has just been completed, and as may be judged by the photograph of her under way which appears on page 47, she is a very attractive ship. By introducing this design, the builders feel they are meeting fairly closely the requirements of the average prospective owner to whom this type of yacht appeals. But, realising that each owner will have his own ideas on matters of accommodation, decoration and equipment, mass production of this cruiser is not intended.

The accommodation has been carefully worked out to make the best use of the available space, the saloon decoration having been designed and carried out by Messrs. Furdecor Ltd. The central steering cockpit, though well sheltered from the weather, is not entirely enclosed ; it is self-draining, and beneath its deck is installed the Thornycroft 6 cylinder compression ignition (Diesel) engine. This engine develops 40 b.h.p. at 1,400 r.p.m., and through 2.1 reduction gear gives a propeller speed of 700 r.p.m. and drives the vessel at about 8 knots.

With the three working sails, a total of 615 sq. ft. of canvas can be set, but a reaching staysail and spinnaker are also supplied. The masts are hollow spars built up of silver spruce, and rigging has been efficiently arranged so that the sails will set properly on a wind and have no tendency to sag.

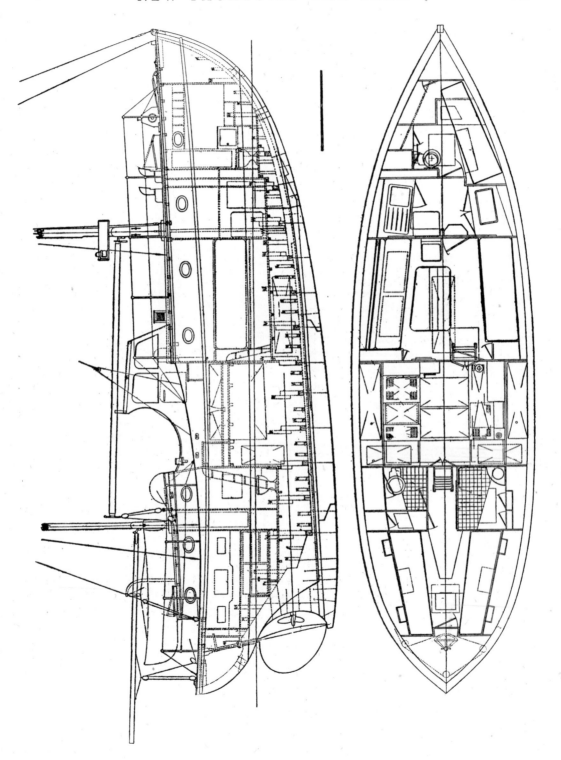

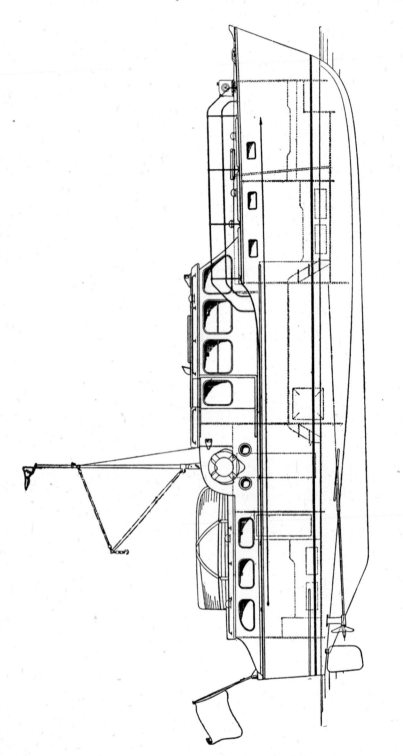

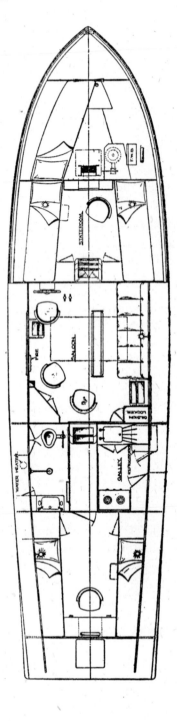

A 42-FOOT MOTOR CRUISER

Designer	.	.	.	John I. Thornycroft and Co., Ltd.
L.O.A.	.	.	.	42 ft.
Beam .	.	.	.	10 ft. 6 in.
Draught	.	.	.	3 ft. 2 in.
Engines	.	.	.	Two Thornycroft 6 cylinder 55–65 h.p. Diesel engines *or* two Thornycroft Ford V.8 type 64–73 b.h.p. petrol engines.
Maximum speed	.	.	.	10–10½ knots.
Cruising range	.	.	.	200 miles, with Diesel engines.
				115 miles, with petrol engines.

WHEN preparing the plans for this new prototype design, three essential considerations were borne in mind : the vessel must be soundly built and seaworthy, her accommodation must be comfortable and she must be economical in operation and maintenance. No attempt has been made to build down to a price ; the aim has been to produce a really well found vessel with high class finish and gear. The price will be in the neighbourhood of £5,400, depending on the type of machinery selected and the final specification.

The designers consider that a length of 42 feet is about the maximum for an owner-skipper to handle, but quarters for a paid hand are arranged right for'ard bulkheaded off from the rest of the accommodation. If a hand is not carried, this space forms a comfortable guest's cabin, so that a party of five can cruise together without any suggestion of overcrowding. The forward double stateroom can be used as a day cabin when required, for it is fitted with settees each side, the backs of which hinge up into a horizontal position to form sleeping berths of good width.

The central feature of the accommodation is the large deck saloon over the sound insulated engine space. This serves also as wheelhouse (the engine controls being led close to the helmsman's position) and dining saloon. With the sliding roof and large drop windows it is a light and airy compartment and an excellent observation place from which to watch everything that is happening in the anchorage or out at sea. As the floor is sunk well below deck level, the tophamper has been kept pleasingly low.

The owner can make his choice between two types of engines : either a pair of Thornycroft 55–65 h.p. six cylinder Diesel engines, or a pair of Thornycroft 64–73 h.p. V.8 petrol engines can be supplied. With a fuel capacity of 150 gallons the yacht with Diesel units will have a 9 knot cruising range of 200 miles and a maximum speed of 10 knots. Fitted with petrol engines an additional half knot can be obtained, and with a cruising speed of 10 knots the range with these units is 115 sea miles.

Sixty gallons of fresh water is carried and this is fed by Bee electric pumping system to the galley and wash basins. A 12 volt charging dynamo is driven by each engine, and in addition there is a ½-kw. Stuart lighting set installed in the engine space.

An 8-foot dinghy with outboard motor is supplied to stow on the cabintop, and a derrick with detachable boom is fitted for handling it.

It is anticipated that delivery of yachts of this type can be made in about six months.

MONA

A 52-foot Fast Cruiser

Designer.	.	John I. Thornycroft and Co., Ltd.
Builder .	.	John I. Thornycroft and Co., Ltd.
Owner .	.	H. E. Ahmed Abboud Pasha.
Engines .	.	Two Thornycroft RL/6 type Diesel engines, each of 130 b.h.p.
L.O.A. .	.	52 *ft.*
Beam .	.	10 *ft.* 6 *in.*
Draught .	.	3 *ft. (approx.).*
Speed .	.	17–18 *knots.*

This vessel has been shipped to Egypt. A photograph of her appears on page 47.

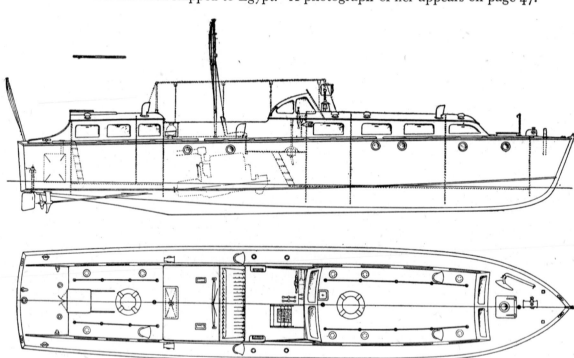

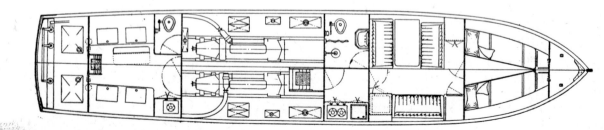

SARACEN

Designer-Owner . Nigel Warington Smyth.
Builder . . G. Percy Mitchel, Port Mellon.
L.O.A. . . 21 *ft.* 3 *in.*
L.W.L. . . 18 *ft.* Draught . . 1 *ft.* 8 *in.*
Beam . . 5 *ft.* 6 *in.* Engine . . 6 *h.p.* Kelvin.

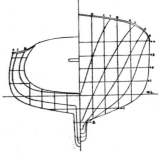

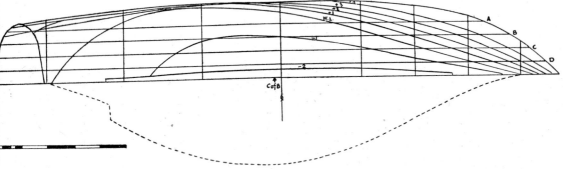

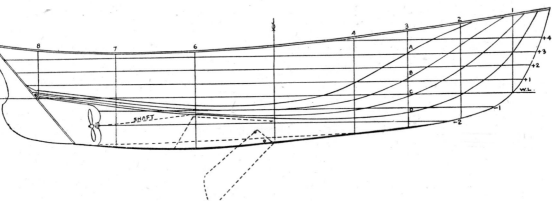

S*ARACEN* was designed primarily for fishing in Falmouth Bay. Dimensions and displacement were dictated to some extent by the fact that a 6 h.p. Kelvin engine with a folding propeller was available for the power installation, and as much speed as was reasonably possible with this power was required. It was therefore decided to go for length and easy lines, with very moderate displacement.

It will be seen that the boat has a long, fine entrance, with a high bow and considerable reverse flare. This makes her wonderfully dry in a headsea. The transom has considerable rake and tumblehome, features which prevent it from having that heavy appearance from which so many " square " sterns suffer.

A small centre-board, housed in the deadwood, enables the boat to sail well under her small dipping lug foresail and standing lug mizen—the traditional Cornish fisherman rig which possesses the great merit of simplicity. Although, of course, primarily a motor boat, sails were considered a necessity in case of engine failure, as the fishing grounds lie some miles off-shore.

A picture of this little vessel appears on page 34.

KATHLEEN ROMA

A Dyco Hawfinch Motor Cruiser

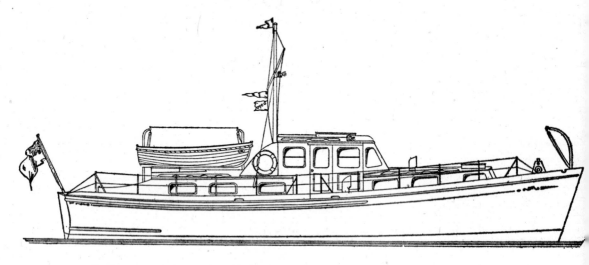

Designer	.	.	.	F. R. Parker, M.I.N.A.
Builder	.	.	.	The Dorset Yacht Co., Ltd., Hamworthy, Poole.
Owner	.	.	.	W. G. Sherren.
L.O.A.	.	.	.	43 ft. 6 in.
L.W.L.	.	.	.	41 ft.
Beam	.	.	.	11 ft. 6 in.
Draught	.	.	.	3 ft. 9 in.
Engines	.	.	.	One or two 65 h.p. Perkins Diesels.

KATHLEEN ROMA is the first of the new Dyco Hawfinch class of motor cruisers to be completed. With her twin screws driven by two 65 h.p. Perkins Diesel engines through 2–1 reduction gear, she can attain a speed of 11 knots.

Two other vessels of the class are under construction at the Dorset Yacht Company's yard to definite orders, but they will be fitted with single propellers driven by engines of the same make and power, and are expected to have a maximum speed of 9½ knots.

Although this is a standard design, owners have a choice of three alternative accommodation arrangements, and can select power units of their own choice. The vessels are planked with mahogany on rock elm or English oak timbers, and mahogany is used extensively throughout the accommodation.

A very complete set of equipment is provided. This includes a 9-foot dinghy, **Calor** gas cooker, fire extinguishers and electrical fittings. The price, without machinery is £3,000, and the present cost of a Perkins P6M 65 h.p. engine is £600.

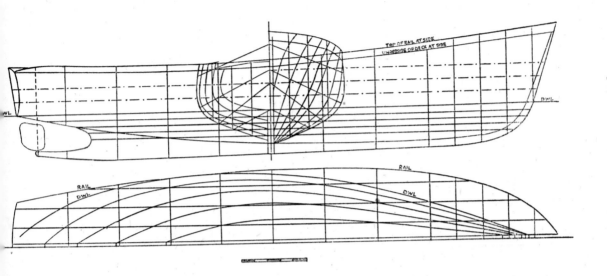

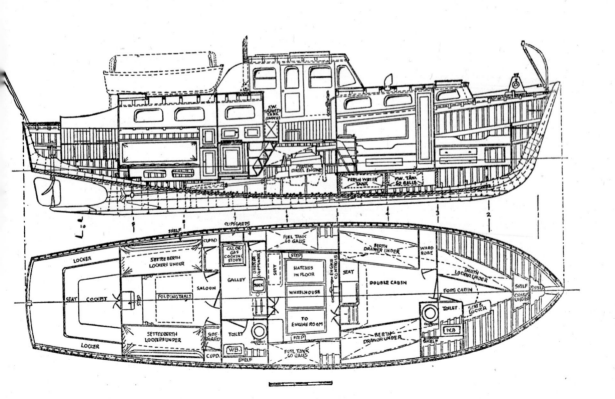

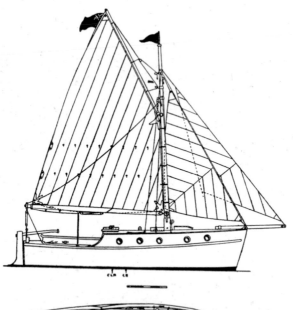

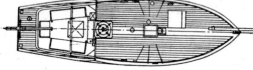

MANA

A 28-foot Motor Cruiser for Fishing and Day Trips

Designer .	.	J. E. H. Tew, A.M.I.N.A.
Builder .	.	R. A. Newman & Sons, Ltd., Poole.
Owner .	.	Gerald Beesly.
L.O.A. .	.	28 *ft.*
Beam .	.	8 *ft.* 2 *in.*
Draught .	.	2 *ft.* 9 *in.*
Engine .	.	4 *cylinder* 20 *h.p.* Dorman Diesel.

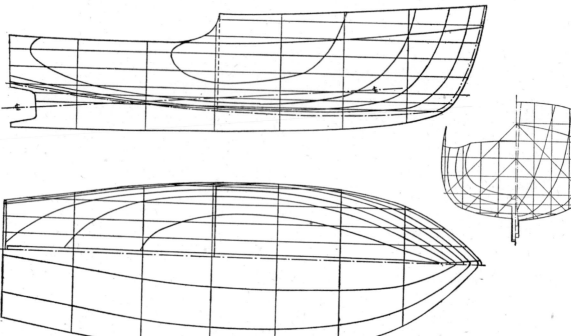

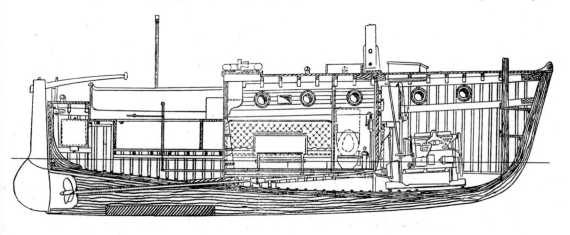

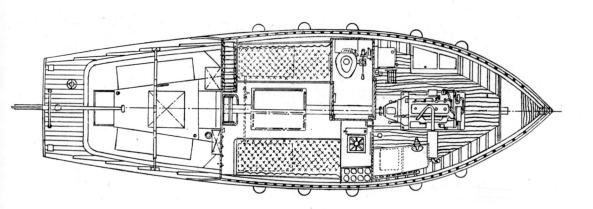

MANA was designed on the general lines of a Poole fishing boat for Mr. Gerald Beesly who required a vessel suitable for fishing and day trips. She was launched from the yard of R. A. Newman & Sons, Ltd., in June.

The forward position of the engine is somewhat unusual, but it has considerable advantages when an owner and his friends wish to spend long periods in the cockpit while under way. With the cabin doors closed the engine can hardly be heard, and in spite of the long propeller shaft there is practically no vibration. As ventilation in all small craft is from aft to for'ard, with the engine in this position any smell from it does not enter the cabin. All controls are, of course, led to the cockpit.

The 20 h.p. Dorman Diesel engine gives the yacht a speed of 7–8 knots, but she also has quite a useful spread of 350 sq. ft. of canvas.

A photograph of her under way appears on page 34.

ALOMA

A 20-foot Motor Cruiser

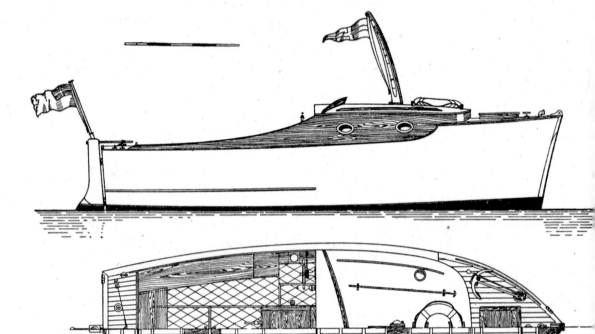

Designer	.	.	.	Harold H. Dawes, A.M.I.N.A.
Builder	.	.	.	Lady Bee, Ltd., Shoreham.
Owner	.	.	.	T. Taylor.
L.O.A.	.	.	.	20 *ft.*
Beam	.	.	.	7 *ft.* 1 *in.*
Draught	.	.	.	2 *ft.* 4 *in.*
Engine	.	.	.	Thornycroft Handybilly, 7/9 *h.p.*

DESIGNED for day cruising, fishing and picnicking, this little motor cruiser was completed in May and proved to be of a generally popular type, simple and comparatively inexpensive to build and maintain, and small enough to manœuvre in restricted places. A sister ship is nearing completion, and it is understood that Lady Bee, Ltd., are standardizing this design.

With the Thornycroft Handybilly engine installed at its for'ard end, the cockpit has ample room for quite a large party, while the little cabin, which is lined and fitted up in mahogany provides a snug retreat when week-end cruising.

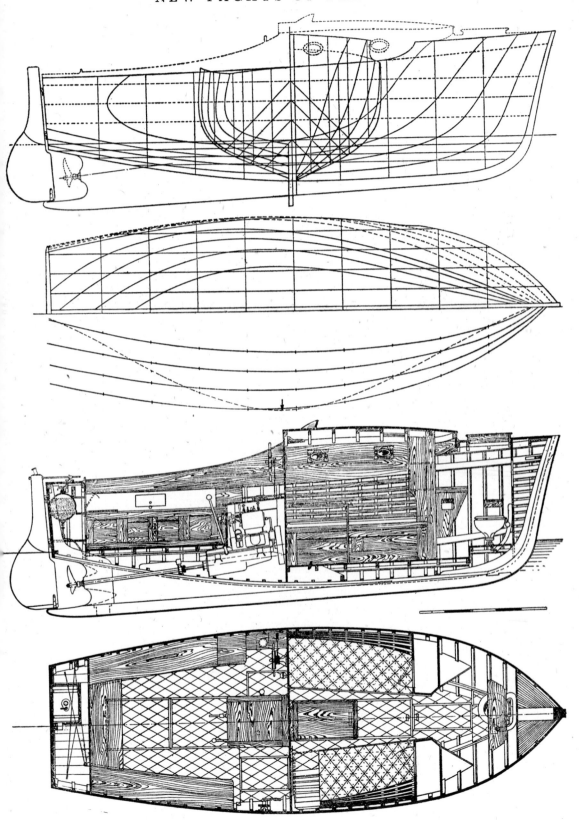

PAX

The first of the *Matelot* half decked week-end "Cruisers"

Designer .	. Kenneth M. Gibbs.	*L.O.A.* .	. 18 *ft.*
Builder .	. Kenneth M. Gibbs &	*L.W.L.* .	. 16 *ft.* 1 *in.*
	Co., Ltd., Shepperton.	*Beam* .	. 5 *ft.* 9 *in.*
Owner .	. G. Harding.	*Draught* .	. 10½ *in.* and 2 *ft. 3in.*

Sail Areas :

·Bermuda	.	. 165 *sq. ft.*
Gunter	.	. 153.5 *sq. ft.*

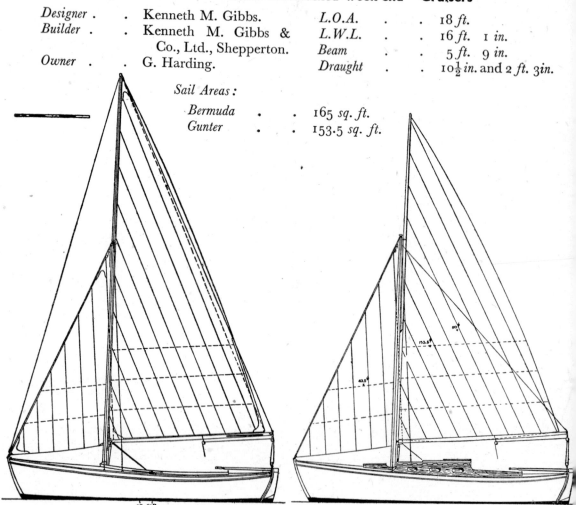

IN 1945 *The Yachtsman* published a series of original designs for half-decked boats with particular emphasis on the following points : simplicity of design and construction combined in a hull that would stand up to rough usage, suitability for day sailing, occasional handicap races and short coastal cruises, and low initial cost and upkeep.

Of this series Mr. Kenneth M. Gibbs' *Matelot* was the most popular, and *Pax*, the first of this class, has already proved to be an excellent little vessel, fast and close-winded, and she does not alter her trim even when heeled to the gunwale. Four more of the type are on order for delivery next season.

The rig may be either bermuda, sliding gunter or lug. We reproduce the first two here, and the gunter is shown over the same hull converted into a diminutive cruiser, as several prospective owners were interested in a permanent cabin. In this case the boat would have built up topsides, giving sitting headroom over the berths, there would be room for a Primus galley aft and a bucket w.c. for'ard.

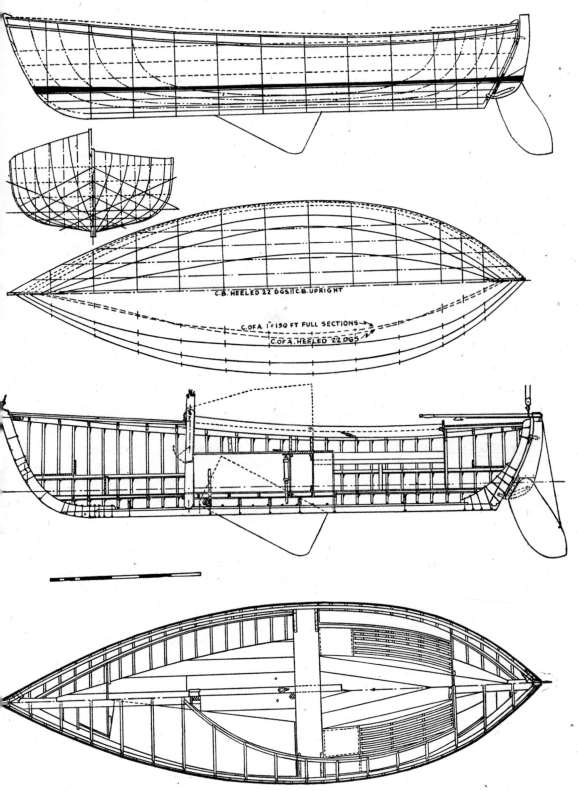

C.B. HEELED 22 DGS. C.B. UPRIGHT

C. OF A. 1=150 FT FULL SECTIONS

C. OF A. HEELED 22 DGS.

H

MUMBLES Y.C.
ONE DESIGN

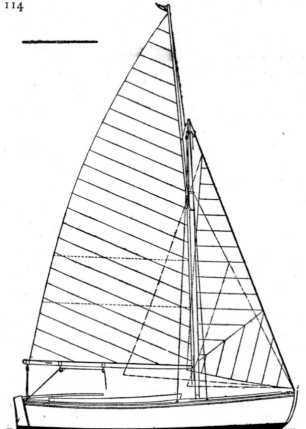

Designer .	.	J. F. d'E. Jones, A.I.N.A.
Builder .	.	David Williams, Ltd., Aberystwyth.
L.O.A. .	.	18 *ft.*
L.W.L. .	.	16 *ft.* 6 *in.*
Beam .	.	6 *ft.* 7¾ *in.*
Draught .	.	1 *ft.* 6 *in.*
Draught with centreboard .		4 *ft.* 6 *in.*
Displacement .		2,620 *lb.*
Iron keel .	.	620 *lb.*
Inside ballast .		400 *lb.*
Sail Area .		174 *sq. ft.*

CONDITIONS at the Mumbles can make life very hard for small craft that are not suited to the locality. Unless they are stoutly built and able to sit upright on the mud, sooner or later they will come to grief lying out in the exposed anchorage.

The designer was asked to produce plans for an inexpensive class boat to meet these requirements. The lines show a hull which is flat of floor and firm of bilge, while the clean waterlines and buttocks should ensure a good turn of speed. The considerable freeboard, the long iron keel and the comparative lack of sheer, all go to make up a vessel which will endure a lot of pounding when sitting upright, and one that will not readily fill even if she gets stuck hove-down on the mud.

The construction plan shows a strong and well knit boat, the centreboard case in particular being very robust. It is secured to logs which are in turn through-bolted to the keel, and its sides are stiffened with floor knees on every alternate timber ; the fore knee is extended to form the mast step. Planking is of ⅝ in. larch on 1 in. × ⅞ in. steam-bent timbers. Three full stringers and one half bilge-stringer add great strength to the hull.

The sail-plan gives ample area and is easily handled, while the boats have enough lateral plane to enable them to go to windward moderately well without the centreboard if need be.

Two of the boats are now building, and it is expected that more will be on the stocks before very long. The design has also been adopted by the Bristol Channel Y.C.

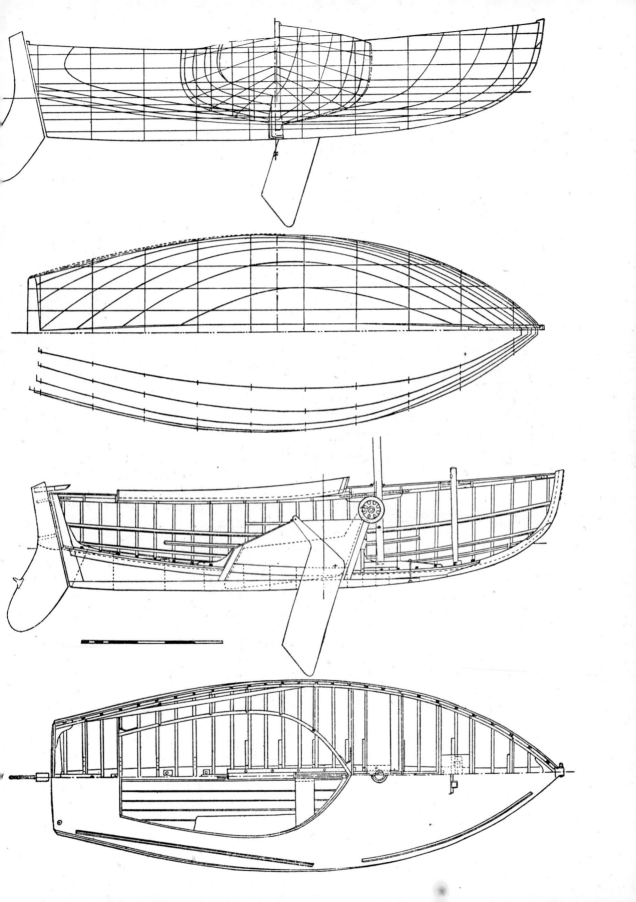

THE YACHTING MONTHLY SHARPIE

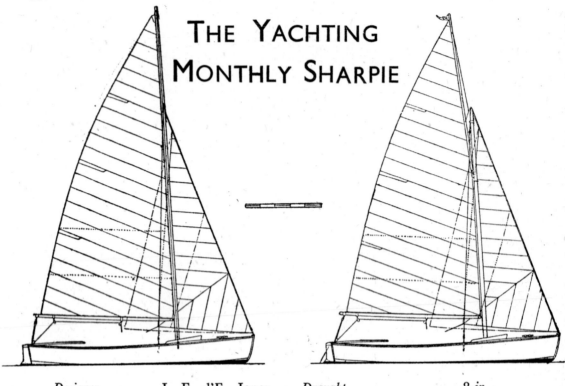

Designer	.	. J. F. d'E. Jones, A.I.N.A.	Draught	.	.	.	8 in.
L.O.A.	.	. 16 ft.	Draught with centreboard	.	3 ft. 8 in.		
L.W.L.	.	. 15 ft.	Weight, hull only	.	.	400 lb.	
Beam	.	. 5.45 ft.	Weight, with crew and gear	900 lb.			
			Sail Area	.	.	.	145 sq. ft.

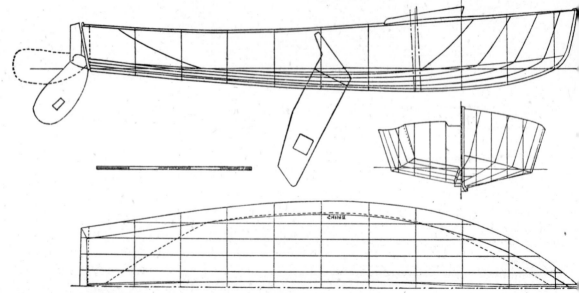

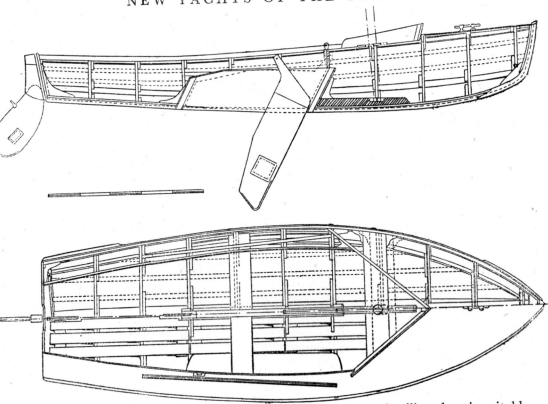

TO meet the growing demand for the plans of a really good sailing sharpie suitable for the inexperienced amateur to build himself, *Yachting Monthly* arranged for Mr. J. F. d'E. Jones to produce this special design, of which prints and notes on building can be obtained from the magazine's London office.

Stores and gear can be stowed beneath the fore-deck, while the side-decks will be of considerable value in choppy water. Both topsides and bottom are so formed as to make for easy planking, whether the orthodox method or waterproof plywood is used. Although the hull construction is sound and strong, the weight of the hull alone does not exceed 400 lbs. This is an important point because a light hull is drier and, other things being equal, is more easily driven than a heavy one, and except in hard winds is often faster. A light hull also has obvious advantages when being moved by road or rail from one place to another, and this one, although she is essentially a sailing craft with a high performance, is light enough to be rowed or driven by a small outboard, for the fitting of which provision is made.

The first of these sharpies to be built by Messrs. Johnson and Jago of Leigh-on-Sea was for Miss K. M. Palmer, Associate Editor of *Yachting Monthly* ; her name is *Willow Wren* and a picture of her appears on page 39. She carries a gunter lug rig which is considered to give a slightly better drive off the wind, though the alternative bermuda sail-plan of the same area should give a little better performance to wind'ard.

The builders have arranged to supply " knock down " parts for building, so that the amateur boatbuilder will be saved much time and wastage of material. A very large number of sets of plans have been sold, and it is understood that many of these sharpies are being built by amateurs in various parts of the world.

THE Y.R.A. NATIONAL 15-FOOT ONE DESIGN

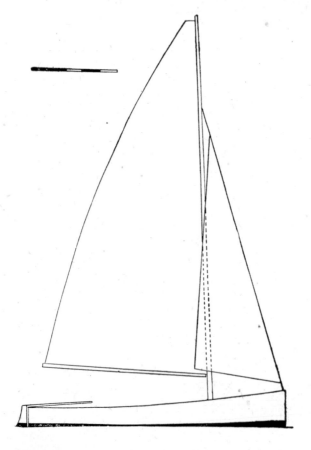

Designer.	.	Uffa Fox.
L.O.A. .	.	15 *ft.*
L.W.L. .	.	14 *ft.* 6 *in.*
Beam (extreme).		5 *ft.*
Beam (waterline)		4 *ft.* 6 *in.*
Draught .	.	8 *in.*
Draught (with C.B.) .	.	4 *ft.* 8 *in.*
Sail Area	.	130 *sq. ft.*

FOR those who require a boat larger than the 12- and 14-footers, the Y.R.A. asked a number of designers to submit plans, and selected one by Uffa Fox.

This boat is, in effect, an enlarged International 14-footer, and because she is a foot longer, it was possible to make the lines cleaner. She is a light, buoyant boat with plenty of freeboard for'ard and good flare to her bows, and she planes readily. Because she can carry a crew of three she has the advantage over the smaller classes of being able to introduce to the sport newcomers with little experience of sailing who may in time become expert and own their own boats.

The sail area is the same as that of the 14-footers, but the jib halyard has been carried 18 inches higher ; this, combined with a 6 inches shorter mast, enables the spar to stand without any topmast rigging above the jib halyard.

We understand that two of these boats will be carried on the quarter deck of H.M.S. *Vanguard* when she sails on her cruise to Africa with the Royal Family.

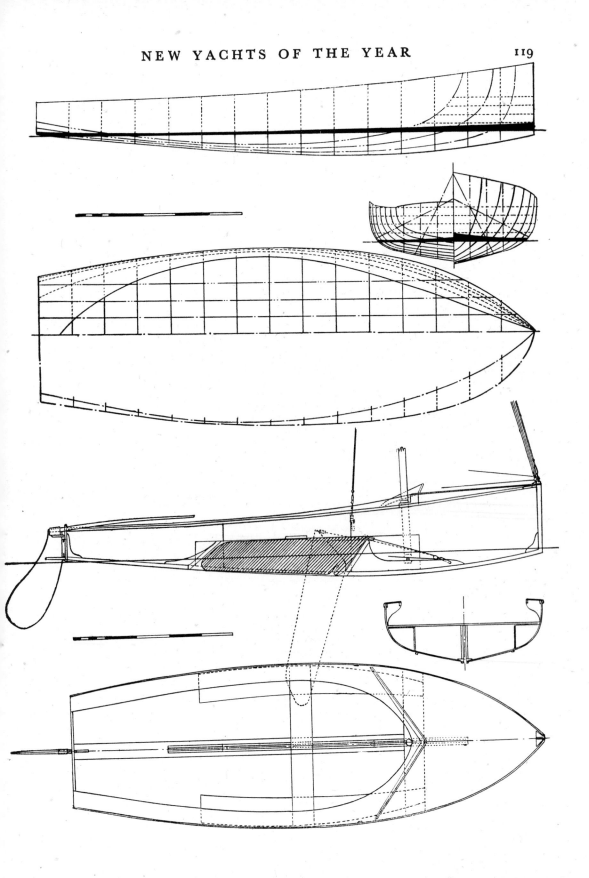

A 15-FOOT HALF-DECKED STOCK DINGHY

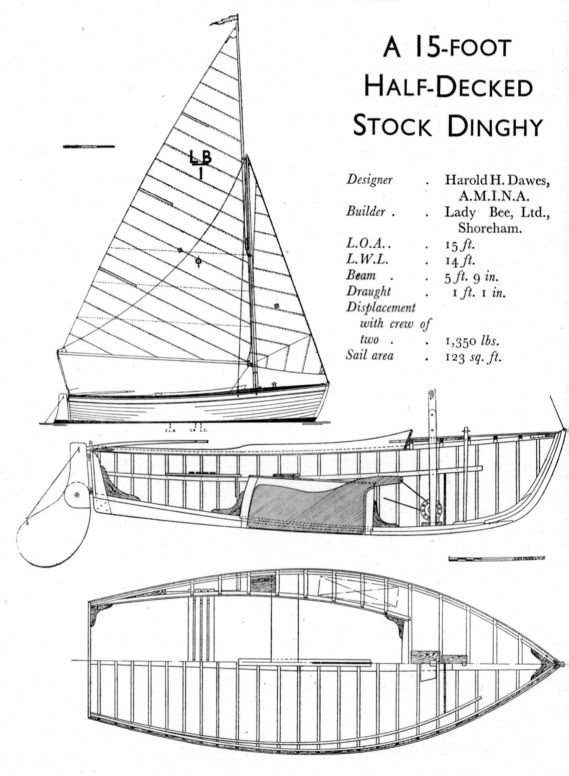

Designer	.	Harold H. Dawes, A.M.I.N.A.
Builder .	.	Lady Bee, Ltd., Shoreham.
L.O.A..	.	15 ft.
L.W.L.	.	14 ft.
Beam .	.	5 ft. 9 in.
Draught	.	1 ft. 1 in.
Displacement with crew of two	.	1,350 lbs.
Sail area	.	123 sq. ft.

THIS half-decked dinghy was designed for a client who wanted a fairly stiff boat suitable for the not-so-young, but capable of giving a good account of herself under sail. When the plans were finished much interest was shown in them, and orders were received for six of these boats ; so it was decided by Lady Bee, Ltd. to standardize the design.

The first to be built, *Lady Bird*, for Miss Perrin of Birdham was delivered in June. The trials were carried out in a strong wind, and the boat proved to be stiff, dry and extremely fast off the wind and she actually planed when running.

Though the gunter rig is convenient for stowing, and the tabernacle is an asset for up-river work, it is proposed to fit future boats with bermuda rig if required.

Laying the planking clinker fashion is simple, cheap and perfectly satisfactory for a boat of this sort, and the general construction to a high specification is robust enough to enable the boats to withstand all the rough treatment to which dinghies are so frequently subjected.

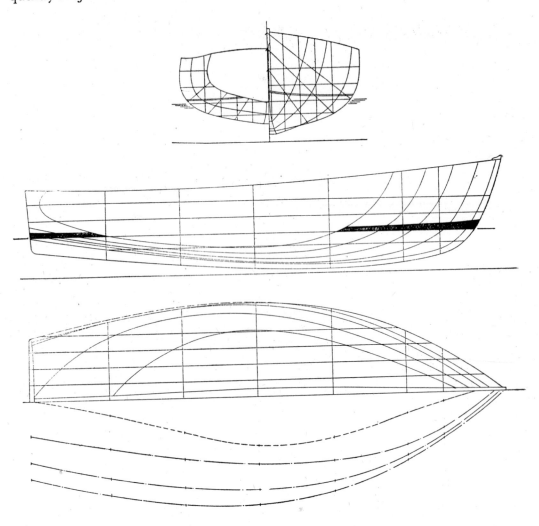

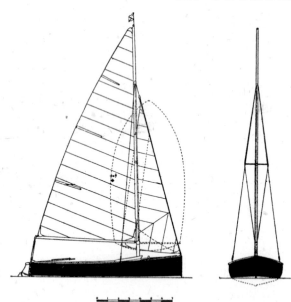

THE I.D.R.A. 14-FOOT ONE DESIGN DINGHY

Designer.	.	O'Brien Kennedy.
L.O.A. .	.	14 ft.
Beam .	.	5 ft.
Draught .	.	8½ in.
Draught with C.B.	.	4 ft. 6 in.
Displacement .		810 lb.
Sail Area .		120 sq. ft.

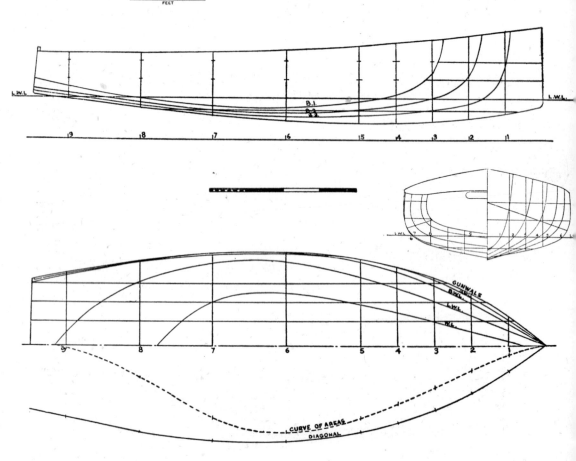

THE first of these boats was designed as a new One Design class for Poole Harbour in 1939, but the war intervened. One boat, however, was built and thoroughly tested during that season. She was raced with great success in handicap events, leaving the field far behind except in the hardest weather, when the bigger ballasted X-boats and Dolphins had the advantage.

Fuss, as she was called, was not designed with speed as the prime consideration, but rather with the idea that she should be a practical day-boat which would really be fun to sail even by comparative beginners. She proved to be safe and serviceable and remarkably stiff.

Since the war the Irish Dinghy Racing Association has shown considerable interest in this boat, and Mr. O'Brien Kennedy modified the design slightly, increasing the sheer as shown in the accompanying plans. The design took Ireland by storm, and 45 of these boats are being built in that country. Fourteen have also been ordered by the Royal Natal Y.C. at Durban, and it is understood that the designer will build these himself for export.

Much thought has been given to the problem of handling and housing these 14-footers on land, and a simple undercarriage has been designed which, if required, can be stowed in the boat when afloat, to be quickly attached and swung down into position when it is desired to haul out of the water, and for road towing.

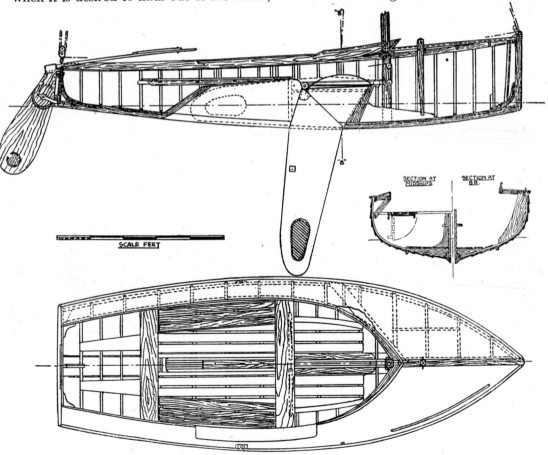

SCALE FEET

SECTION AT MIDSHIPS   SECTION AT B.B.

THE Y.R.A. NATIONAL 12-FOOT ONE DESIGN

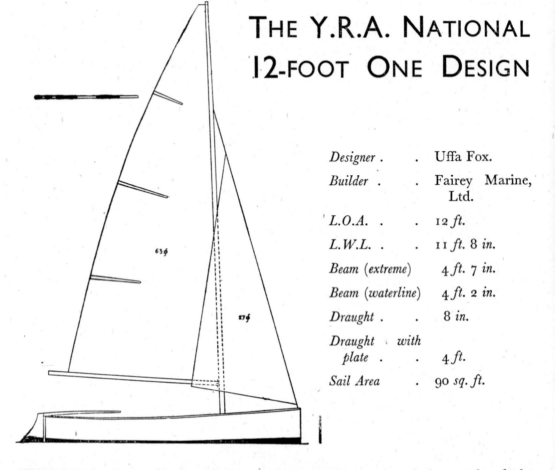

Designer .	.	Uffa Fox.
Builder .	.	Fairey Marine, Ltd.
L.O.A. .	.	12 *ft.*
L.W.L. .	.	11 *ft.* 8 *in.*
Beam (extreme)		4 *ft.* 7 *in.*
Beam (waterline)		4 *ft.* 2 *in.*
Draught .	.	8 *in.*
Draught with plate .	.	4 *ft.*
Sail Area	.	90 *sq. ft.*

WHEN, immediately after the war, the Yacht Racing Association explored the possibility of a National 12-foot One Design Class, they studied all the existing classes and boats, and came to the conclusion that the Cambridge 12-footer was the best, for while being designed to the National 12-foot rule, she was also designed to be a stable boat suitable for undergraduates to serve their apprenticeship in.

To produce a high quality boat of this sort at a low price, the Y.R.A. took the bold step of deciding on moulded plywood construction and production by a single firm, Fairey Marine of Hayes, Middlesex, a firm new to the boat building industry. The hull is only ⅜ in. thick and is built up of nine plies of birch veneer laid alternately in a horizontal and vertical direction.

Compared with the old 12-footer, the new boat has a firmer bilge, flatter floors and nearly 5 inches more beam on the waterline, so she is more stable and easier to handle. But in spite of those differences and because of her light weight, she has proved to be the faster boat. Both mast and boom are of light alloy with metal sleeves to take the bolt-ropes of the sails, and the mast is a foot shorter so that it may stand without topmast rigging of any kind.

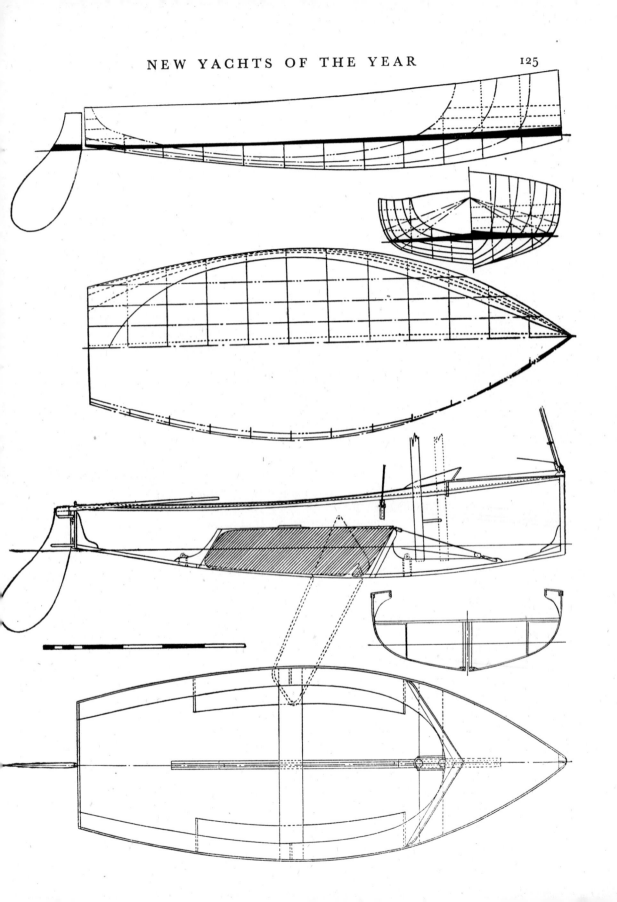

THE DEVELOPMENT OF SHOAL-DRAUGHT

By MAURICE GRIFFITHS, G.M., A.I.N.A.

Editor of *The Yachting Monthly*

FROM the time of the Civil War for well nigh fifty years a battle was fought in America between the advocates of the centreboard and the " cutter cranks." Whilst neither side can ever claim to have won a victory over the other, the effect of the arguments that ranged up and down the Union and brought echoes even from the far off Solent, has been a marked modification of the ideas of both schools of thought, and a general compromise.

The great stretches of sheltered water in North America, the broad shallow rivers and the land-locked sounds where small boats can sail, naturally enough encouraged a type of sailing boat with very limited draught. The drop-keel or centreboard was, indeed, an American invention of early Colonial days, and as it enabled even flat bottomed boats to sail close-hauled, its use soon became almost universal for all classes of sailing craft. Until the 1860's boats for private sailing or for inland water transport in America, were in consequence mainly flat-bottomed or of such shoal draught that a centreboard was an essential part of their equipment. The early shalop, the piragua, the New York flat boat, the Chesapeake bugeye, the Hampton flattie, the cat boat, the New Haven sharpie and many of the coastal schooners were all shoal draught craft with large wooden centreboards to help them beat to windward.

Few of these boats carried inside ballast, but the racing cat boats used for private match sailing carried moveable sandbags for ballast which were piled on the weather deck, and in the more spectacular races capsizes were quite common.

It was only amongst the big ocean going yachts, the schooners of the very wealthy before the era of the steam yacht came in, that vessels with deep hulls and heavy draught were to be found in the American continent.

In England, on the other hand, those very conditions that favoured the shoal-draught centreboard type so much in America hardly existed for the Victorian yachtsman. Those areas of shallow seas and creeks and rivers which have since become yachtsmen's cruising grounds—the Essex rivers, Chichester Harbour, Poole Harbour, the Dee and Morecambe Bay, the Humber, the Trent and the Norfolk Broads—were almost unknown to the yachtsman of the 1860's. What little yachting was done was confined chiefly to the Solent or the Firth of Clyde and, for the larger yachts, to cruises up and down Channel and across the Irish Sea.

Under these conditions the English yacht for both racing and cruising had to be a deep water boat suitable for head-winds and generally hard weather conditions. The earliest yachts naturally enough followed the lines of the naval despatch boats, the revenue cutters, the deep sea smacks and the cutter rigged packet boats.

Deep, massively built hulls of peg top section were the order of the day, with all the ballast stowed inside. To drive these heavy displacement yachts enormous sail plans with heavy spars and long topmasts and bowsprits were common, and, to complete the vicious circle, to give them stability to stand up under this press of rigging and canvas, a great weight of ballast had to be stowed below the floorboards.

As the old bluff bows gave way to the finer, wedge-shaped cutwater, and the earlier cod's-head-mackerel-tail model became lengthened into a slimmer, more sea-kindly form, stability became a problem. With sharper garboards and less and less beam, succeeding yachts needed greater depth of hull and more ballast to enable them to carry their sail. To bring the weight as low as possible, ballast was taken from the inside and cast on the keel, tentatively at first, until the time came when all the ballast was bolted to the bottom of the keel.

This tendency to build yachts deeper and heavier with less and less beam was aggravated as one rating rule after another placed a penalty on beam throughout the 1860's and 1870's until it culminated in the infamous Length and Sail Area rule of 1880—1886 that produced the deepest and narrowest yachts of all time, the "plank-on-edge lead mines." (Fig. 1). It needed but the wreck of the 10-tonner *Oona*, which was driven ashore in a gale on the Irish Coast when her 10 ton keel dropped off and her crew of four perished, to check this deplorable fashion for excessively deep, heavily-ballasted and narrow yachts. But in yachting customs die slowly, and the belief that a yacht must have a deep and heavy keel appendage to go to sea is still widely held in this country.

In America, where the development had been in precisely the opposite direction, namely in the direction of the broad, shallow centreboard craft, even for some of the largest yachts, it also needed a disaster or two to check a tendency towards excess. The capsize of the 100 ft. centreboard schooner *Mohawk*, which was struck by a sudden squall in 1876 while she was at anchor with her sails sheeted in, and several persons, including some ladies, were drowned, drew public attention to this dangerous possibility of the broad, flat-type of yacht—the tendency to capsize. (Fig. 2).

There were already many advocates of what had come to be known as the English cutter type, the non-capsizable, deep, narrow craft with ballast both inside and on the keel. The equally staunch supporters of the American broad centreboard type

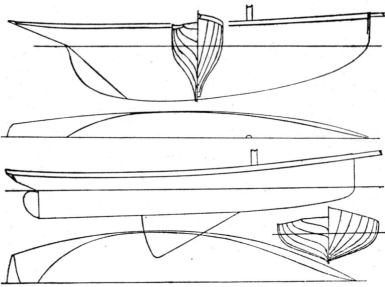

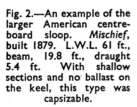

Fig. 1.—A good example of the "plank-on-edge" yacht was *Clara* designed by Will Fife, Jr. in 1884 for the 20-ton class. L.O.A. 63.75 ft., L.W.L. 52.75 ft., beam 9 ft., draught 9.8 ft. Displacement 37 tons. All ballast, 22 tons of lead, on the keel.

Fig. 2.—An example of the larger American centre-board sloop. *Mischief*, built 1879. L.W.L. 61 ft., beam, 19.8 ft., draught 5.4 ft. With shallow sections and no ballast on the keel, this type was capsizable.

called them " cutter cranks," and the arguments between the two factions resounded up and down the United States with vituperation on both sides. The cutter cranks held that the narrow English type was the only safe craft to go to sea, for whatever the weather, however steep the seas might become, these yachts would not capsize. (Fig. 3).

The advocates of the broad and shallow types, on the other hand, held that most yacht owners spent all, or very nearly all, their sailing days in comparatively sheltered waters, where a wedge-sectioned yacht with a deep draught would be quite unsuitable. A beamy craft with light draught for sailing into the more popular anchorages, they argued, was of infinitely greater use to the average yachtsman, and did not require anything like the weight of gear, or spread of canvas to drive her. The difference in the amount of gear aloft between the deep draught cutter yacht and the centreboard sloop was as great then as that between a gaff cutter and a bermuda sloop today.

The arguments of the centreboard enthusiasts on behalf of the seaworthiness of the shoal-draught type were given considerable fillip by the great blizzard that swept in from the Atlantic across New York State in 1888, and caught two yachts at sea making the passage south. One of these was the 100 ft. yawl *Cythera*, a plank-on-edge English-built vessel of great displacement, a fine example of the sea going type advocated by the contemporary cutter cranks. The other was the *Whim*, a 63 ft. Yankee-built centreboard schooner. When the blizzard had passed the *Whim* was given up for lost, for no vessel but the staunchest, deep draught type, it was felt, could survive such a hurricane. But to everyone's surprise the 63 ft. *Whim* came in, while after many days of suspense the 100 ft. *Cythera* was given up for lost. The story the crew of the *Whim* had to tell was of getting their sails down before they blew out of the bolt ropes and of riding tremendous seas under bare poles with the centreboard hauled up. Making considerable leeway the yacht left a " slick " or swathe

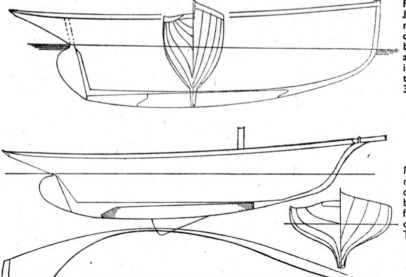

Fig. 3.—*Surf*, designed by John Harvey in 1883, was modelled on the " English cutter " type. All the ballast was on the keel and the yacht was peculiar in having no reverse curve to her sections. L.W.L. 35.3 ft., beam 7.6 ft., draught 7.4 ft.

Fig. 4.—The " compromise " type of keel-centreboard sloop is shown by *Nymph*, built in 1888 for the 40-foot class to designs by Edward Burgess. This type was non-capsizable.

of smooth water to windward, which effectively prevented the crests from breaking and catching hold of her. Retreating from their anger she was too elusive to allow any water other than spindrift from breaking over her. The plight of the *Cythera*, which was never heard of again, could well be imagined, and the centreboarders lost no opportunity in driving it home to their cutter rivals. With her narrow heavy hull held fimly from making leeway by the great depth of the keel, the plank-on-edge yawl would lie like a half-tide rock in the water, unable to "give" to the seas, and offering herself to the full fury of their onslaught. The *Cythera* was not the only vessel to be lost at sea in the next few decades through having too deep a draught and too heavy a displacement.

Whilst the more extreme advocates of the English cutter cried "You'll capsize in your unseaworthy skimming dishes," and the centreboarders retorted "You'll be washed overboard and drowned from your lead mines," yacht designing was becoming a more widely recognized profession, and through the untiring efforts of such designers as the Fifes (father and son), G. L. Watson, J. M. Soper, Arthur Payne and Dixon Kemp in Great Britain, and Edward Burgess, Beavor Webb, Nat Herreshoff and others in the United States, a more moderate and shapely form of both opposed types was being developed.

The day of the "plank-on-edge" yacht was over and the era of what came to be known as the Britannia type just beginning. A more moderate type of centreboard yacht had been developed at the same time and was known as the "compromise sloop." Not so broad nor so shallow as the earlier catboats and racing sloops, the hull had easier sections with a moderate rise to the garboards and a ballast keel through which the wooden centreboard worked. This type was indeed a compromise between the earlier centreboarders and the orthodox keel yacht, and whilst possessing better windward qualities than the earlier skimming dish hulls, she was also more sea-kindly. The most notable improvement was, however, that like the true keel yachts she was non-capsizable. (Fig. 4).

At last, therefore, before the turn of the nineteenth century, an admirable compromise had been arrived at between the skimming dish and the lead mine. Since then yacht designing has developed along reasonable lines in America in producing both the normal deep keel cruising and racing yacht, and the equally satisfactory shoal draught yacht with a modest keel and a centreboard.

From this brief resumé it will be seen how different was the yachting background of the two countries. Whereas the American yachtsman had grown up to accept centreboard yachts as a major part of the yachting scene, in England there had been no call for this shoal-draught type. English yachtsmen and yacht designers were steeped in the cult of the deep and narrow form of yacht for both racing and cruising. It was not, in fact, until the railway reached Burnham-on-Crouch in 1888, and such places as Brightlingsea, West Mersea, Pin Mill, and Aldeburgh, familiar enough to us now, first became yachting centres and opened up the whole of the Thames Estuary as a small boat's cruising ground, that the need for a shoal-draught yacht was recognised. With the appearance of yachts in Poole Harbour, Morecambe Bay, Hoylake, the Humber and the Trent, yachtsmen began to build small craft that could make use of tidal harbours, slip into shallow creeks, and take the ground without damaging their bilges.

The American idea of a shallow hull with plenty of beam for stability and a

I

drop keel or centreboard to help the boat to windward, seemed to be the obvious answer. Unfortunately there were no naval architects in England concerned with this type of small yacht, and the construction of these early centreboard boats was left entirely to the local builder, who had had no experience of the type.

The result was as may be imagined. There was already a deep prejudice in English yachtsmen's minds against any form of Yankee yacht that did not follow the deep keeled English model and, particularly against that Colonial invention, the centreboard. No good, it was felt, would come of cutting a slot down the very backbone of a yacht, her oak keel, and making a board slide up and down inside it. The whole contrivance was too much like another of those smart dodges of the Yankees designed to cheat something or someone, and not proper for an honest-to-God British-built yacht.

Thumbing over his own conception of what a " centreboard b'ot " should be like, with all his distrust for any novelty, the regular British boat builder got it into his head that the board was there not so much to give adequate lateral area—to add to the surface below water, in fact, to check leeway— but to increase stability. " It's a keel, a drop keel, ain't it ? " was the apparently logical argument. These iron or steel centreboards—some were to be bronze and actually weighted at the lower end with lead—introduced an era of strains and leaks, of bucklings and broken hoisting tackle and profanity that had been happily free from the easily worked wooden boards of the American boats. All the simple lore of the *wooden* leeboards, so long used in Holland and by the Thames spritsail barges, the Cowes ketches and a host of other types of commercial craft in Europe, was ignored. The English builder decided that a centreboard was an iron or bronze drop keel, and needed to be as heavy as possible, and so in this country it became.

The fact that a centreboard does not alter the stability, or power to carry sail, of a yacht is not generally understood. Only in the smallest boats, such as the International 14-footers and 12's, can the lowering of the deep and heavy metal plate be said to increase stability to any worth-while degree. In a yacht of 20 ft. waterline or more, the additional stiffness caused by lowering even a heavy iron or yellow metal plate is inappreciable.

This custom of thinking a centreboard should necessarily be a metal plate has been confined almost solely to British boat builders and yachtsmen, and its acceptance has caused much avoidable trouble in boats so fitted. In Holland, and in the Thames barge, leeboards, having the same function as a centreboard, have been used for centuries—they are, in fact, the oldest form of adjustable lateral resistance. Yet no one has heard of any botter, boeier, hengst, hoogaarts, tjalk, lemsteraak or other Netherlands craft with *iron* leeboards, nor to my knowledge has any Thames barge, whether wood or iron built, had anything but the orthodox wooden leeboards. Iron leeboards would be altogether too heavy to work and too liable when hitting the ground to plough in.

For this and other reasons a centreboard of wood is greatly preferable to a metal plate ; it is far lighter and easier to work, it will skate over the mud and not dig its lower edge in, it will not wring so that it cannot return into its case, and it can be chamfered or streamlined to offer the least resistance. The board may be built up of oak or teak planks—the board in my own 25 ft. W. L. *Lone Gull* is made up of 2 in.

oak through-bolted with an iron strip along the lower edge to make it just sink—or it may be laminated with a $\frac{1}{8}$ in. iron plate betwen 1 in. planks, or again it may be cut solid from 9 or 13 ply resin bonded plywood, such as " Resweld," in which case it will need little or no extra weight to make it sink.

In English yards at first there was much to be learnt, too, about the best methods of installing the centreboard case, so that it should neither weaken the hull nor be liable to undue strains and leaks. A century of practice had developed simple and strong forms of centreboard case in the United States, where in coasting schooners up to as much as 120 ft., in many of which two centreboards were fitted, the cases formed such a rigid part of the construction as to take the place of keelsons and added strength to the hull. It followed that the early attempts at the drop-keel type of small cruising boat in England were full of snags and troubles, and by reason of their faulty construction and the ignorance displayed by builders and owners alike on the elementary essentials of centreboard installations, strained cases, buckled plates and the inevitable leak became synonymous in English yachtsmen's minds with the devilish contrivance. In another book, *Little Ships and Shoal Waters* (Peter Davies Ltd., 21s.) I have given examples of centreboard case construction which need not reappear here.

Even today, after more than half a century of centreboard yacht building in this country, we often see builders and designers planning a centreboard installation for a client, with the same old faults reproduced all over again. For instance :

(a) There is the centreboard made of $\frac{5}{8}$-in. mild steel plate that required an elaborate and expensive winch or a cumbersome tackle to raise it.

(b) There is the plate that, when down, leaves too little of its upper part inside the case and so gets wrung and refuses to come up again.

(c) There is the large iron plate that is too thin for its area or becomes rusted away and bends when the yacht hits the ground while making some leeway over the mud. Once a plate is bent or wrung and refuses to return into its keel slot or case, there is nothing for it but to have the crippled vessel hauled out on a slip and the plate removed.

(d) There is the plate with such small clearance in the keel slot that after soft mud and fine sand have been forced in and become packed until the plate will not budge, there is no room to work an iron lath or saw blade down between plate and case to clear it.

(e) There is the plate that cannot be got at without putting the ship on the hard or slipway merely to free it of shells, mud and stones—a common enough experience with centreboards when the yacht regularly takes the ground at moorings.

(f) There is the lifting tackle, cunningly concealed perhaps in a polished brass tube, that sooner or later breaks and cannot be attended to without pulling half the yacht's cabin to pieces.

(g) There is, more often than not, the plate that has no form of stop on it, and sooner or later when the tackle carries away or is accidentally let go with a run, drops right down, to hang vertically below the keel on its pivot bolt, and get permanently wrung as soon as the yacht begins to sail or touches the ground.

Before planning a centreboard installation in a new design, therefore, it may be as well to enumerate the following conditions which are considered essential for satisfactory working :—

(1) The case must be so substantial and through-bolted as to form a very rigid structure and act as a keelson ;

(2) Any joints in the case or the case log should be accessible inside for caulking ;

(3) Part at least of the case should be above the load waterline so that it can be quickly opened up, while the yacht is afloat, for freeing the board of mud, shells or stones ;

(4) The slot in the keel and case should be not less than ¾-in. wider than the board. Experience has shown such ample clearance is necessary for a completely free-operating board under all conditions of service, and for clearing the board of mud etc. with splines or iron laths ;

(5) The chain or wire lifting tackle should be accessible for immediate examination or replacement while afloat ;

(6) The board should be fitted with a form of stop to prevent it from being able to drop below its normal sailing position. If the tackle parts or is let go altogether the board should drop only onto its stop ;

(7) When lowered to its stop, or sailing position, there should be enough area of the board left inside the keel slot and case to take all the lateral strains imposed on the board by leeway, beating in heavy seas, running aground etc.

(8) The board should never be too heavy to haul up easily by a light crab winch or tackle ;

(9) It should be possible to withdraw the board without having to pull the yacht to pieces.

To these requirements I should also like to add a general one on centreboard cruising yacht design, namely, that the vessel should be designed so that if the centreboard is temporarily stuck right up in its case and it is necessary to get the ship underway, she should be able to sail and to beat to windward, if only in an indifferent fashion, without her board. The point is important, for there are occasions when perhaps a stone has jammed the board in its case, the tide is falling and there is not enough time to open up the case and free the board. If your vessel is so flat that she will sail only crab fashion without her board, then you may well have to miss a tide, or risk getting into trouble with a boat that will not stay or turn to windward.

Many years ago, back in 1922 or '23, I had a 24 ft. centreboard sloop which was then a fairly old boat and had the general sections and flat floor of a large dinghy. She had no outside ballast, but a rusty iron plate working through a false keel which was only 3 in. beneath the garboards. She would sit upright on the ground, of course, and float in 2 ft. of water, but she boasted pretty nearly all the possible faults of a drop-keel boat. Yet I enjoyed sailing her. With her plate up she was helpless except in blowing to leeward, and on one occasion I had reason to curse this failing, for I was anchored over the mud on a falling tide with the plate apparently firmly rusted in the case and the wind backing and coming on shore. An upleasant situation.

To build a boat of some 5 tons T.M., on the general form of a dinghy is, of course, a mistake, for the minor faults of the dinghy are magnified in the larger edition. The full round sections and abrupt run at the stern make for sluggishness in light breezes and a devilish hard mouth when it blows ; the extreme shallow draught in spite of a fairly large area of plate, makes poor windward performance ; and finally in a boat of this form, however initially stiff her flat sections may make her, as in a small barge, if she heels beyond a certain angle there is a real danger of her capsizing.

This boat and her successor a year later, a 22 ft. racing sloop with a hutch-like cabin and an enormous iron centreplate that at first could scarcely be raised or lowered and finally rusted solid in the iron keel slot, showed me how bad and troublesome such craft could be. Wherever one went one heard the same complaints about centre-board boats : jammed plates, leaking cases, sodden bedding and clammy, smelly cabins. It was this general acceptance of what seemed to me logically avoidable that induced me twenty years ago to study the development and design of shoal draught.

In the earlier boats built to my designs, I fitted ⅜-in. mild steel centreplates of a type based on the late Albert Strange's. In this the plate was like a clasp-knife with an open blade, or L-shaped, pivoted so that the tip of the blade worked along a slot in the deck. Albert Strange adopted yawl rig and placed his mainmast well forward, so that the slot for the centreplate arm lay between the mast and the cabin top. (Fig. 5). This necessitated placing the mast, in my way of thinking, too far forward for sloop or cutter rig, and in three of my earliest boats, *Wind Song*, 26 ft., *Caravel* 30 ft. and *Loon* 30 ft., the mast was stepped in a tabernacle whose members were bolted through the after part of this case. (Fig. 6.) Whilst this enabled the mast to be stepped in its

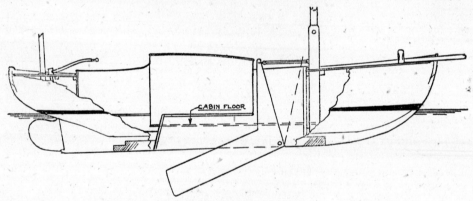

Fig. 5.—Method of fitting L-shaped centreplate in small yacht, introduced by the late Albert Strange.

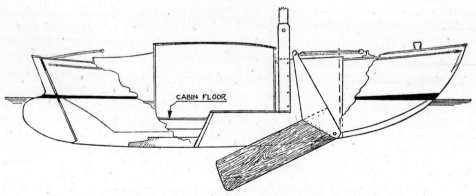

Fig. 6.—An alternative position for mast and L-shaped centreboard in a sloop or cutter This places the centreboard farther for'ard.

proper place, well back in the ship, it resulted in the centreplate being rather too far forward, a fault which I discovered in the majority of contemporary yachts. If the yacht did not carry lee helm with the plate up, when it was lowered she would become very hard-mouthed. It seemed to me that it was desirable to place the centreboard so that the yacht's centre of lateral resistance or trim would not move either forward or aft appreciably whether the board was raised or lowered.

The L-shaped centreboard seemed to me to have advantages over the rectangular or triangular plate of early days, for the arm with its lifting gear was clear of the waterline when hauled up, and when lowered there was plenty of the plate or board left in the case to bear the side thrusts.

In an attempt to bring the C.L.R. of the centreboard when lowered directly below the C.L.R. of the hull when heeled and sailing, in the next design I placed the L-shaped centreplate much farther aft with its arm and lifting gear in an extension of the case at the after end. Still copying English practice and not yet aware of the advantages of a wooden board, I made the centreplate of ⅜-in. mild steel. *Ayuthia*, 45 ft. ketch built by native labour in Siam, was an example of this practice.

This type of installation was found to work well, for the case extension at the after end could be carried to the deck beams and so made completely rigid, (Fig. 7), and it could be opened up by means of a quickly removable panel for inspection of the centreboard or for clearing the case of mud and stones. With the forward part of the case flush with the cabin floor, forming in fact a very solid section to the cabin sole, and the galley, lavatory, or small engine room worked in to one side of the extension case, it was possible for visitors to come aboard, as they do in my own ship *Lone Gull*, and not notice that she has a centreboard.

It only needed what I ought to have realized years before—the fitting of a properly shaped wooden board in place of the heavy steel plate, to make the presence of a centreboard almost trouble-free and the whole contrivance easy to operate, effective, and an excellent sounding device !

There still remained the development of the hull design which too often in the past had been derived from the sailing dinghy or "longshoreman's punt." The possibility

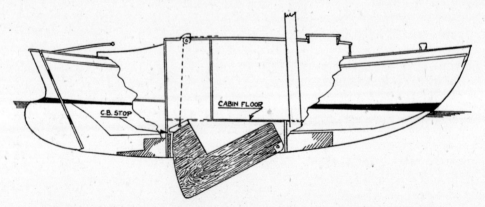

Fig. 7.—A wooden centreboard with its case flush with the cabin sole. A stop prevents the board from being lowered too far. The after (extended) part of the case opens above the waterline for inspection.

of capsize, I felt, should be eliminated altogether, and in later designs I drew up stability data to ensure an ample safety factor in case the yacht is knocked down by a squall. It will be remembered how in America the cutter-cranks' main arguments against the centreboard craft were their possibility of capsizing, and how by developing a somewhat deeper model with a moderate ballast keel, the " compromise sloop " type was evolved which could take a knock-down, and still right herself. This I consider an essential requirement in any seagoing shoal draught yacht, whether she is fitted with a centreboard or not, and in recent designs I have worked in certain ratios of depth of hull, beam, draught, rise of floor, keel weight and other minor factors which will ensure the required stability.

The once popular belief held by yachtsmen in this country and by cutter-cranks on the other side of the Atlantic, that a shoal draught yacht could never be fit to make sea passages, is on the wane. Whilst many cruising men express the opinion " I like plenty of boat under me when I go to sea," meaning that they feel happier with a deep keel under them, it is in fact only a personal preference. Provided a vessel of shoal draught (with a shallow fixed keel or a centreboard) is non-capsizable she should prove as safe a boat at sea as the deepest draught yacht.

Long voyages have been made in all sorts of weather by sailing craft with draught less than one-half of their beam. For instance a crew of Estonians recently sailed from their country to New York in a koster boat, a double-ended clinker-built cutter 37 ft. by 14 ft. with a fixed draught of only 3 ft. 6 in., encountering plenty of hard weather and heavy seas. Slocum's famous world-sailing *Spray* was a shallow craft with 13 ft. 10 in. beam and but 4 ft. draught, and my old friend Henry Howard has always declared his 52 ft. C.B. ketch *Alice* (designed by a designer of U.S.A. lifeboats which she resembles) was safer and more comfortable at sea than any deep-draught, heavy displacement yacht. The *Alice* measures 13.7 ft. beam and 4 ft. draught, and has a plain wooden centreboard substantially fitted according to our list of nine rules. And as she has cruised for many years up and down between Rhode Island and Florida, and about the West Indies, and has ridden out a number of gales in deep water, her owner who has long experience with all types ought to know a seaboat.

If the advocates of heavily ballasted hulls and deep keels for seaworthiness are entirely right, it might be said that there is not a *lifeboat* throughout the world fit to be put to sea : for I have yet to meet either a ship's boat or a shore-launching life-boat with tons of ballast and a deep keel. Yet I believe it is generally accepted that lifeboats are known to survive rough seas and indeed to put out into storms when bigger and deeper craft need their help.

Therefore, where local conditions, such as a harbour that dries out or an anchorage with all the deepwater berths taken, call for a yacht with very limited draught—less than half the beam—there is no reason why a perfectly satisfactory cruising boat should not be designed and built. She should be able to take advantage of the shallow water berths or the creeks that nearly dry out. and yet prove an able seaboat when it comes to making a deep water passage. A happy compromise, in fact.

WORK YOUR WINDS

By L. LUARD

(CDR. W. B. LUARD, O.B.E., R.N., RETD.)

FAIR winds and foul are all in the day's work when cruising or racing. Though many have learnt to get the best out of a ship from aspects such as trim, set, sheeting and handling of sails, and tension of rigging, as well as from the art of sailing to windward in all weather conditions, few have studied the effects of shifts of wind, anticipated or unexpected, upon relative and actual positions.

It is an interesting subject and worth while. Used with some skill, and perhaps more luck, it can send the winning flag aloft, particularly when conditions enforce a considerable amount of beating ; used with common sense, it can save unnecessary nights out when passage making ; used with a flair for local forecasting, which is often more reliable than broadcast weather reports (anyway this summer), it helps to bring that confidence and assurance every seaman should possess.

The central concept of all windward strategy is based on the bow bearing of the mark, finishing line or destination in relation to the ship's sailing angle to the true wind, and to the varying changes in this angle through shifts of wind, sudden or anticipated.

The problem to be solved, therefore, is to produce a simple instrument that shows the loss or gain resulting from sudden shifts, and the ideal position to be in to take full advantage of anticipated shifts. It is not a difficult matter. In point of fact, it is a very simple one for ships that sail at a fixed angle to the true wind when beating. Unfortunately this is never the case, and complications at once arise ; for apart from every ship sailing at her best at different angles to the true wind in varying weather conditions—this angle also being affected by leeway and tidal stream—ships of different type sail at different angles in the same weather conditions. In other words, an infinitely variable indicator is necessary.

First, however, it is better to show the construction of a fixed indicator, and the varying stages that go to its completion. In Fig. 1 the distance sailed to make good 6.4 miles dead to windward is ten miles, the angle made good to the true wind being 50°. Thus the distance a ship must sail to make good a given distance dead to windward, or up wind, varies as the secant of the ship's angle to the true wind. Conversely, the distance made good up wind for a given distance sailed, varies as the cosine of the ship's angle made good to the true wind.

These two generic formulæ are the foundation upon which everything is built. To make this matter quite clear, a follow up diagram (Fig. 2) shows that the distance sailed from point C to any point on the line E.B. is the same as the length of the line C.B. or C.E. whether one tack is made or a dozen, as long as the ship's angle made good to the true wind is the same on both tacks.

Thus a ship tacks at D or G to make A

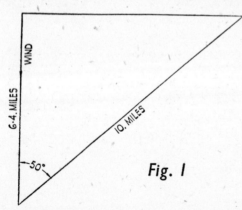

Fig. 1

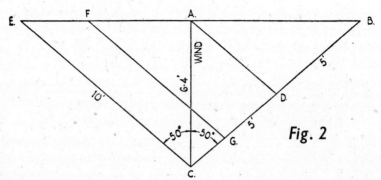

Fig. 2

or F. But the triangles A D B and F G B, are isosceles, A D being equal to D B, and F G to G B. This means that if one line is drawn through the ship's position to represent the direction of the wind, and another at right angles to the wind line through the destination, any point on the second line, within the two tacking courses, is equidistant from the ship.

Fig. 3 shows an application of this simple fact in practice. Any point on the line V T is equal in distance from the ship's position at A. In heavy weather, with darkness folding in, port T, as opposed to port Y, is an obvious choice, the influence of a weather shore being progressively felt, one of those dispensations that make the end of a hard thrash to windward so delightful. A situation of this nature often occurs when cruising, and is worth bearing in mind.

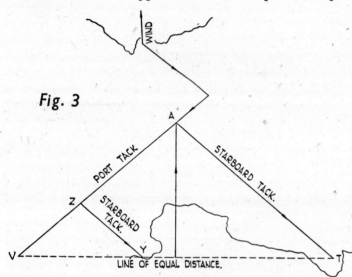

Fig. 3

The next step is to see the effect of shifts of wind when beating. In Fig. 4, the mark B' bears 20° on the port bow, the ship making good 50° from the true wind. Thus a freeing wind shift of 20° lets her lay C B' direct, if she is on the port tack. On the starboard tack, B' would bear 80° on the bow, and the wind would have to free that amount to let her shape direct on the line C B'. However, if the wind heads 80°, with the ship on the port tack, or 20° when she is on the starboard tack, the result is the same —she at once goes about and shapes direct for the mark B' along C B'.

A rule can now be drawn up for anticipated shifts of wind. With a freeing wind the bearing of the destination on the bow must equal the shift ; with a heading wind,

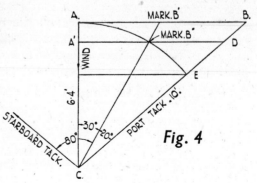

Fig. 4

the bearing, added to the shift, must equal the ship's sailing angle to the true wind ; or, more simply, the bearing of the destination on the bow must equal the tacking angle (100° in these examples) minus the anticipated shift.

Fig. 4 shows the effect of a shift of wind. A 50° ship that has the mark dead to windward, distant 6.4 miles, has 10 miles to sail (C B). But if the wind shifts 30° at this precise moment, her sailing distance is decreased by the length B D ; and if it shifts 50° by the length B E.

Another example from the same Fig. shows the effect if the mark is not dead to windward. It is now assumed to be at B'', 6.4 miles 20° on the port bow. A fair or freeing shift of this amount would therefore decrease her total sailing distance from C D to C E, that is by an amount D E.

The relative gains and losses can be calculated mathematically. With the mark 20° on the bow, 6.4 miles (C B'', Fig. 4), the distance to sail is 6.4 × secant 50° × cosine (50–20°) miles. With the bearing 80° on the bow, the cosine element becomes 80–50°. The position is seen at a glance. The length C D is required, C B'' being known. In the right-angled triangle C A' D, the length C A' must first be found, when C D can at once be solved.

The final stage in the composition of a fixed windward diagram is shown in Fig. 5. For convenience, the mark is kept fixed and the ship moved—the right way to go about things. The mark B is 6.4 miles dead to windward of E. Thus C A E D is a line of equal distance, B A and B C being 10 miles, a 50° ship, situated anywhere on this line, having 10 miles to sail to reach B. A ship at A makes B—for example—in two tacks, A G and G B, or A X and X B—equal to B D or B C.

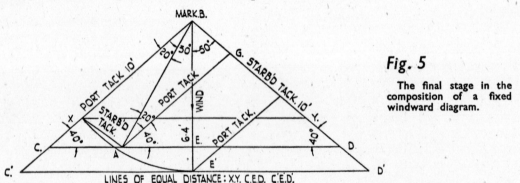

Fig. 5

The final stage in the composition of a fixed windward diagram.

However, at A, on the port tack, the mark bears 20° on the port bow, or 80° on the bow for the starboard tack ; and a fair shift of 20° (refer to rule) at once lets her shape along the line A B, which swung on the radius to X, shows that the distance sailed is X B instead of C B, a saving in distance of CX ; and X Y has now become the new line of equal distance.

With a foul shift of 30°, the ship is transferred to E', dead to leeward of her destination, and has to sail a distance C' B, an increase of C' C. The completion of a fixed tacking diagram is now in sight—an amplification of the triangle C' B D', with lines drawn parallel to C' B and D' B for port and starboard tacks, and lines of equal distance added, for the scale chosen (its units can represent cables, miles, or tens of miles),

supplemented by circular arcs, and pecked lines that identify the bearing of the mark
on the bow.

Fig. 6 shows one in its simplest form, and a few examples make its use clear. The
ship, on the port tack, is 9 miles dead to leeward of her destination. This, by following the 9-mile arc, puts her on the 14-mile line of equal distance at A—her distance to
sail. If the wind heads 30°, the bearing of the mark or destination on the bow is now
80°, and the ship has moved to the 12-mile equal distance line (A 1), and has, therefore,
saved 2 miles. If she is headed 50°, the mark bears 100° on the bow, and the ship
moves to the 9-mile equal distance line (A2) on the limiting port tack line, with a saving
of 5 miles. She goes about and makes direct for the mark. A similar freeing wind
brings identical gains on the port side of the diagram—B1 and B2.

Another example shows the ideal line of bearing to make for anticipated shifts.
The ship is again 9 miles dead to leeward of the mark, and sooner or later a heading
shift of 30° is predicted. She must therefore make for the line of bearing bringing the
mark 70° on the port bow (C) [tacking angle minus anticipated shift], and ladder up
this line in short boards until the shift arrives. If the wind, true to form, heads her
on arrival at C, she has $7\frac{1}{4}$ miles to sail instead of $10\frac{3}{4}$, and even if this be delayed,
she is on the right line of bearing, for the short tacking policy.

Had, however, a freeing shift of 30° been anticipated, when she was dead to leeward of the mark, she would make for the line of bearing, that puts it 30° on the bow for

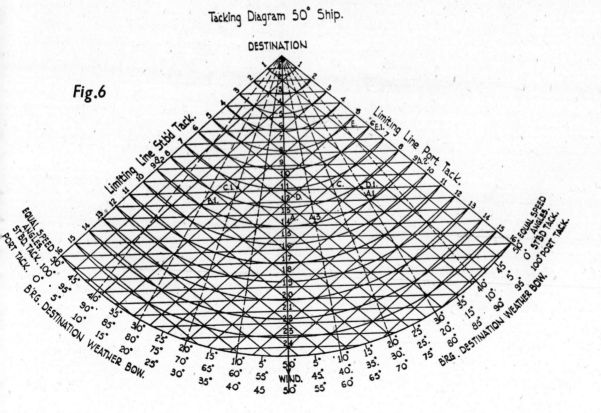

Tacking Diagram 50° Ship.

Fig.6

DESTINATION

the port tack, or 70° on the bow for the starboard one (C1), pursuing similar laddering tactics until the wind obliged. Counting the grid squares gives the distance to sail to reach this ideal position.

Unfortunately a fixed tacking diagram is more theoretical than practical; for the variation in the sailing angle made good to the true wind is at the mercy of leeway and tidal stream and the state of the sea, quite apart from vagaries of helmsmanship, that cannot be discounted, except by the remark that anyone who mishandles the living beauty of a ship deserves all the misfortunes lack of skill and understanding bring. But it is only another step to design a variable diagram that takes all but the human factor into account, and this is shown in Fig. 7.

Here, the port and starboard tacking lines, or grid, can be adjusted to the angle made good on each tack to the true wind; and a leeway indicator is provided, as well

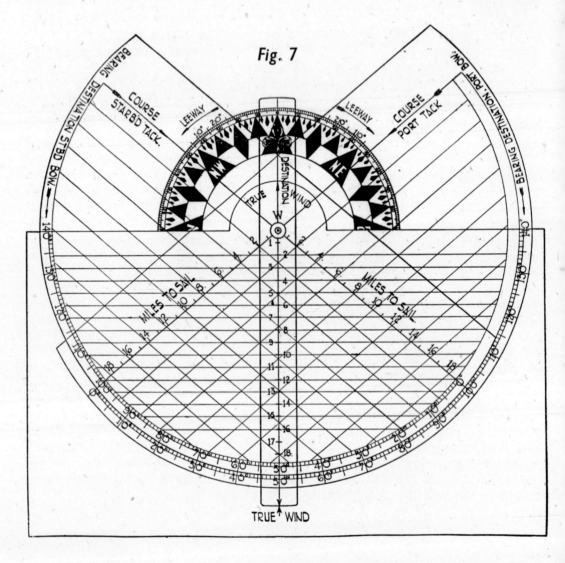

Fig. 7

as a compass, and a pivoted, scaled arm that dispenses with the circular arcs, and the figures on the lines of equal distance. All problems can be solved, either as bearings on the bow, or as compass bearings. Vector triangles can also be resolved so that the effect of tidal streams can be compensated without use of the chart. It is, at present, the most advanced solution a friend and myself have been able to achieve in a simple, cheap form, and it will be manufactured, it is hoped, in time for the coming season.

Certain fundamental rules of windward tactics can now be summarized. A ship dead to leeward of her mark gains on any shift of wind. If the shift equals her sailing angle made good to the true wind, the distance to sail to reach the mark becomes the actual distance she is away. With a greater shift, she at once frees sheets. Small shifts of wind, with the ship dead to leeward of the mark, give small gains in distance compared with similar fair ones when she is near her limiting tacking lines. Conversely, foul ones of the same degree bring identical losses.

A ship gains most when the shift places her so that she can lay the mark direct ; she loses most if a foul shift takes place when she is on her final tacking line, gaining nothing but freed sheets, and an increase of speed, if the shift is fair. Finally, with the bow bearing of the mark greater than the ship's sailing angle made good to the true wind, a heading shift is always fair, a freeing shift, unless large, foul, the reverse being the case when the bow bearing of the mark is less than the ship's sailing angle to the true wind.

For example, with the mark 80° 9 miles on the port bow, a heading shift of 20° places a ship on her final tacking line, as already shown—A1 to A2, with a saving of three miles. A similar freeing shift brings her to A3, with 4.75 miles more to sail. Actually a freeing shift of 80° would be necessary to equalize the 20° heading one, and another of 60° to keep her sailing distance to the mark unchanged. It is, therefore, vitally important to be in the correct sector for anticipated shifts, and to make for the line of bearing that gives the greatest gain in distance.

The indicator can also solve equal speed problems ; and Fig. 6 is the easier diagram to give examples in print (though its angles are limited). When sailing dead down wind, for instance, at 7 knots, what increase of speed is necessary to tack to leeward with a divergence of 30° on each gybe ? Follow the 7-mile arc to the central line at D, then swing back 30° (from equal speed angle figures), when the answer is found to be about 8.2 knots (D1). The same principle can be applied for windward work, and a theoretical example is shown in Fig. 6 again (because there is not space to make a special drawing of the variable indicator set for a practical problem). A ship sailing at 5 knots, and making good 40° from the true wind, has to increase her speed to 6 knots to cover the same distance up wind in the same time, if her sailing angle becomes 50° —E to E1.

The elements of windward work have only been touched. The effect of tidal streams on apparent wind brings many interesting problems that determine tactics. Others, too, where the dividing line between close-hauled work and sailing free are closely related can all be solved, besides tacking to leeward ones, which are the handmaiden of light and moderate weather. Though the wind bloweth where it listeth, some knowledge of countering its vagaries is an important factor in winning races, inshore or offshore, and is as important for the cruising man.

YACHTING HAS NO NATIONAL BODY

By THE EDITOR of YACHTING WORLD

RECENT events have indicated only too clearly the need for the early formation of a national representative body for British yachting, and for some time past I have been advocating in the columns of *Yachting World* the formation of such an organisation. Certain of the more active and far-seeing clubs have taken up the matter, but I do not think that the majority of yachtsmen realize how very important it is for their interests to be in the hands of some virile national association.

Since the war, both in certain sections of the yacht-building trade and amongst certain harbour and other authorities, there has been a trend towards a tidying-up of their relations with yachtsmen. This has resulted in proposals, some of which have been far from acceptable by the latter as a whole and, while there has been a great outcry from individuals the bodies responsible have found no association either of yachtsmen or clubs with which they could negotiate. Their feeling is naturally one of frustration, and they may well decide, as in the case of a mooring and storage agreement, that any arrangement, though it may have its defects from the yachtsman's point of view, is better than none at all.

There are other problems connected with the trade, such as the right of the owner or his crew to work on laid-up yachts, which has yet to be settled, while the question of mooring charges also arises, for those adopted by the Southampton Harbour Board, if they become general, will add a great deal to the cost of yachting. On the face of it, they seem to be very high, but so far as I am aware, I am the only one to have challenged them.

Quite apart from the militant aspect of such an organisation there are many ways in which it could render service to yachtsmen. We do not perhaps want anything quite like the A.A. or the R.A.C., but there are many ways in which help could be given in connection with cruising. At home in many of our favourite haunts, facilities even for going ashore, are sadly lacking, possibly because no one has ever pointed out the need for them, while the publication of an authoritative handbook which would be kept continually up to date by a live organisation would solve many a yachtsman's problems. A great many yachtsmen will undoubtedly want to visit the continent during the forthcoming years and the formation of some central authority to deal with foreign cruising will become more urgent as time goes on. Judging by the ever increasing volume of letters and telephonic inquiries with which my office deals every day, there is also a crying need for a comprehensive information bureau qualified to deal with every conceivable aspect of yachting.

Argentine yachtsmen recently desired to express their appreciation of the magnificent work done by British yachtsmen at Dunkirk, and the Argentine clubs combined to send a token of their esteem. They waited on the British Naval Attaché in Buenos Aires, and the question immediately arose as to what body in this country should receive it. In his dilemma, the attaché solved the problem on the spot by forwarding it to the Royal Yacht Squadron, as the senior British club. This was, of course, but a compromise, for it should have gone to a national body had there been one to receive it.

One of the many difficulties in forming an association of this kind is finance. Obviously it can be made partly self-supporting, but a certain amount of money will be required especially in the initial stages. An approach was therefore made by a number of prominent yachtsmen to the Yacht Racing Association, which is the only existing national yachting organisation and which already has a financial link with practically all British clubs, to ask its members whether they would widen their constitution to embrace other interests. The Y.R.A. is inclined to consider this proposal in a favourable light and a sub-committee of the Council has been formed, under the able chairmanship of Mr. F. G. Mitchell, Commodore of the Royal Corinthian Y.C., to consider the proposal, and there the matter rests at the moment.

I cannot impress too strongly upon yachtsmen in general and upon club committees in particular, the need, in these times, for authoratitive and effective representation, otherwise they may find all sorts of impositions and irksome regulations inflicted upon them. The utility aspect of such an organisation must not be overlooked, and is equally important for it may well become by far the biggest side of its activities.

THE YACHT RACING ASSOCIATION
By THE SECRETARY, Y.R.A.

THE YACHT RACING ASSOCIATION was kept alive and in order during the war years, thanks largely to the good offices of the Hon. Treasurer, Mr. Algernon Maudslay, C.B.E., who assumed the duties of Acting Hon. Secretary at that most difficult time.

The late Secretary, Major B. Heckstall-Smith, after a trying illness died in 1943, having been in office for 46 years, and within the next 12 months the Council, under the Presidency of Major Sir Ralph Gore, Bt., began to prepare for what would undoubtedly prove a very responsible task : the reconstruction of yachting in the post-war years on a democratic basis, which would be adaptable to all incomes and so encourage the maximum number of people to learn how to sail a boat.

New offices were acquired at 54, Victoria Street, Westminster, and Mr. F. P. Usborne was appointed permanent whole-time Secretary, as it was the wish of the Council that a Secretary should at all times be available there to reply to letters and to answer telephone calls from anyone who might require information. This facility has already been exploited by many yachtsmen, including those anxious to make a start, also by visitors from abroad and by the press.

The re-measurements of all yachts of the 6-metre Class has progressed and certificates of rating have been issued. The Council have ruled that all dinghies requiring certificates of rating must be re-measured and the appointments of Y.R.A. Official Dinghy Measurers over a wide area have been confirmed ; 150 certificates have been issued.

Two new one-design dinghies of moulded ply construction have been introduced : the Y.R.A. National 12-footer and the Y.R.A. National 15-footer. Many hundreds of the smaller type have already been sold and the inquiry for the larger boat promises to be even greater from both home and overseas buyers. (Uffa Fox designs were chosen for both these classes which are being built by Fairey Marine Ltd. Their plans appear on pages 118 and 124.—Ed.)

Many new 14-ft. International Dinghies have been built and the entry of 59 boats for the Prince of Wales Cup Race, under the auspices of the Brixham Yacht Club, being larger in 1946 than ever before. Similarly, the 12-ft. National Dinghy Class is steadily increasing and interest is active in the 18-ft. National Dinghy Class ; these pre-war classes alone totalling over 1,000 boats.

The rules of all the dinghy classes are shortly to be examined, with the co-operation of all yacht clubs interested in the matter.

A larger racing yacht with 200 sq. ft. of sail area will shortly be introduced and it is hoped will be in quantity production for the 1947 season.

The revision of the *Y.R.A. Handbook* is in progress and will include an examination of the racing rules for submission to the International Yacht Racing Union, at the Union's first post-war meeting this year.

Handicap racing has proved exceedingly difficult in the 1946 season, due to the shortage of crews and condition of gear, but the Y.R.A. intend to encourage these classes on a basis adaptable to post-war conditions.

The Council, with the active co-operation of interested concerns, successfully represented to the Government the resentment of all yachtsmen regarding the proposed imposition of a purchase tax on yachts, with the result that the tax was abandoned, to the great advantage of the trade and buyers who had rightly anticipated a further inflation of values.

The Association has received many requests to enlarge the scope of its activities by acting as a National authority for all yachtsmen and these requests are receiving the Council's most serious consideration.

Plans are already in the making for the operation of the XIVth Olympiad (Yachting Section) in 1948, and all indications point to the most rapid revival of yacht racing, with more boats and more personnel interested than have ever been seen before in any part of the world.

New yacht clubs continue to seek recognition by the National authority and it is becoming more generally known that election to private membership of the Y.R.A. is available to all those who are interested in the expansion of yacht racing in its widest sense.

Editor's Note

AS we go to press we have further news of the larger racing yacht mentioned in the above article, showing that the Council of the Y.R.A. is fully alive to the problems of yachtsmen and is endeavouring to solve them. The Small Keel Class Committee, composed of Y.R.A. Council Members, asked for designs for a new keel class with 200 sq. ft. of canvas. Of those submitted, one from the board of Morgan Giles was considered to be the best and is now under construction. Uffa Fox is building one to the design of Tom Thornycroft, and it is hoped in the latter half of November to stage a series of races in the Solent between these boats and another designed by Air Commodore Chemier. As a check on seaworthiness and speed, a Dragon and a Redwing will also take part.

The new class is intended to be fast and weatherly and to cost not more than £350, just half the present price of a Dragon.

THE CLYDE FORTNIGHT

By IAN G. GILCHRIST, A.R.P.S.

Illustrations by the Author.

" G'BYE Darling," called the owner's wife.

" 'Bye," replied the dripping figure, as he struggled to button up the oilskin round his betowelled throat.

" And *do* try to keep dry," she added.

" Yes," he answered flatly, and made for the club launch and his 6-metre, adding inwardly, " What a hope ! " Another owner followed, with similar wifely injunctions, leaving the two wives—usually amongst their respective crews—to catch the next steamer home. They'd had enough of it in this sort of weather. At the first two regattas it had been bad enough, but this again, for the sixth, was the limit.

Such was the trend of the conversation as I stood amongst a little knot of owners and crews by McCreath's office on Hunter's Quay pier. Such was the weather at 10.15 a.m. on Thursday, 4th July, and the first race was due to start in 45 minutes' time, under the stewardship of the Royal Western Y.C.

We were trying to shelter as best we could from the soaking nor'-easter which was driving in vicious squalls across the mouth of the loch and up the cobbled pier towards us.

For a fleeting moment Strone Hill stood out in clear patches of green and brown, relatively bright against the lowering sky above Loch Long. As the first of the Eights, under main, and genoa in stops, ventured out past *Zigeuner*, the Commodore vessel, to take a look at the line and a smell of the wind outside, we began to speculate on the possibilities of the weather improving. The wind had now eased off a bit and this slight break in the lowest layer of nimbus seemed, perhaps, to herald a general clearing. But it soon closed in again, as thick as ever, and the rain found its way a little farther down our necks.

The third, fourth, and fifth regattas had been held in very fair conditions, and, though the weather had never looked really settled, it might have continued to make amends for the opening day, when, out of 25 starters, only 15 finished, whilst on the next day, when conditions were even worse, only 14 out of 27 finished. Thus it was that today's return to these filthy conditions had come as such a bitter disappointment that at least those two wives had backed out in disgust.

Yet, it was on this very day that the fleet of Dragons had risen from a mere baker's dozen (pre-war) in the earlier regattas, to its peak total of 21 starters. And this may well be taken as a general indication of the keenness noticeable throughout this first post-war Clyde Fortnight.

There had been practical difficulties enough in holding the event at all this year, but the gales at the start were doubly unfortunate. It is bad enough, in normal times, to have to risk ones spars in a gale right at the beginning. Few would have minded taking the same risks at the end, but, with pre-war gear of doubtful condition (and most of it irreplaceable at that), it was particularly unfortunate that the greatest tests should have come in the first two regattas.

I thought it was especially hard luck in the case of one owner, Walter Bergius, who had just taken delivery of his fine 20-ton sloop, *Chameleon*, and turned out on the opening day to race with the " over 20-tonners." When gybing round the first weather mark her mainsail tore from leach to luff. Next day, thanks to the all-out work of McKenzie's, she turned out again, only to tear it once more in another place. However, as by that time her two opponents, *Cymbeline* and *Noreine* had retired, she carried on under jib only and took the prize. But, like *Vagrant*, the ex-8-metre, who tore her mainsail before the start, she did not actually race again—and who could blame her ?

However, lest this account may seem to paint too gloomy a picture of the Fortnight, I must hasten to add that the Firth did smile again, and conditions were quite perfect at the end.

Monday, 1st July, the second of the Royal Clyde's fixtures, was the first of the good days. A moderate southerly breeze, with long periods of sunshine, made the Firth look her old self again. Of course it would be idle to say that the scene was quite up to pre-war standard, for there were none of the fine " big yawls," so characteristic of the Clyde, which usually headed the programmes in the over 60 tons (handicap) class ; and it must have been a disappointment to many of the older generation to see none with jack-yarders in consequence. Even Dr. J. P. Leckie's 51-year-old fiddle-bowed cutter *Panther*,who carried her jack-yarder as lightly in all weathers as she did her years, was absent this year, though still going strong as a cruiser. Dr. Leckie was now sailing his German-built ex-12-metre, *Cymbeline*, the scratch boat, and the largest of the fleet. She had to allow *Noreine* and *Chameleon* 25 seconds per mile each, and succeeded in saving her time twice, out of five starts.

" . . . she charged along our weather side with a hissing roar." *Noreine*, the Anker-built 25-tonner, was the most consistent starter in her class.

With the damage to *Chameleon*, and *Noreine* being often the only other starter in the " over 20's," and because of similar conditions in the " under 20's," the two classes were sometimes combined. Both were dominated by *Amita*, the ex-8-metre whose new owner, Mostyn Vicars, had brought her back to familiar waters from the Menai Straits. She showed in no uncertain fashion that, though now fitted out for passage-making and sporting an R.O.R.C. number, she had lost little of her old form. The result was, that though *Noreine* was the most consistent starter in her own class, she often had to take second place to *Amita* even when the scratch boat was absent. Indeed *Amita* was putting up such a good show that she was sent away with the class Eights one day, and that was the only race she did *not* win. She therefore swept the board, both in and out of her class, with 6 firsts out of 7 starts.

On the day I obtained the accompanying photo of *Noreine*, *Amita* was leading this lovely Anker sloop by a good mile or so. We were lying in wait off Lunderston Bay. As *Noreine* approached us the wind freshened somewhat ; under the press of her huge masthead jib she was well down to the rail, and fairly smoking along. She came at us like an express train, her hefty dark blue hull and powerful bow showing up the bone in her teeth and frothy wash in brilliant contrast (though the sun was, at that time, obscured). As she charged along our weather side with a hissing roar, her long low coachroof and wide side decks gave me a great impression of her weight and power, which I had not appreciated from a distance. Then we opened our throttle. As she still drew ahead and we fell off along her quarter wave, I noticed (between moments of wiping the spray off my lens) that her helm was just a fraction of a degree to weather of amidships.

When she went about to fetch the mark we were surprised to find how long she took to gather full way again. That big jib took some handling with a crew of only four amateurs, and Mr. Lang, her owner, had to keep it a-shiver for some moments while they got the last few inches in on the sheet. But when she was let draw again, she dipped her rail, the roar and foam increased, and one could almost feel the terrific driving power of that sail as the heavy ship visibly accelerated until, once more, she was full and by.

When *Noreine* had rounded the mark, after a little pinching at the last, we throttled back again to watch her set her spinnaker which was giving a spot of bother. When it was eventually cleared and its silky folds billowed out aloft, we noticed a small tear, about the size of a Ratsey's " peephole." It was then that the small boy of a Dragon owner exclaimed, pointing at the " hole," " Look ! *that's* why she's going so slowly ! "

If the handicap classes were somewhat irregular in composition and turnout, the five Eights were the opposite.

Four of the five Eights which turned out regularly Helen, Felma, Sagitta and Sappho, just after the start of the Royal Northern Y.C.'s regatta on 6th July

HELTER SKELTER.

Johan leading *Erica* on a broad reach off Kirn at the first of the Royal Northern Y.C.'s two regattas. These were the only two Sixes to take part in the Clyde Fortnight.

Though many boats were late afloat this year and the total of the fleet did not reach its peak of 46 starters until near the end in consequence, the Eights have been up to full strength from the opening regatta in May, with scarcely an absentee (excluding evening matches) throughout.

Consequently, there has been some very good sport and the picture of their general form is easily completed. A. W. Steven's *Felma* emerged triumphant, after some close tussles with Sir Thomas Glen-Coats' *Pandora*, and D. H. and F. N. G. Taylor's *Sappho*. *Felma* had 4 firsts against *Pandora's* two, and they both had 2 second flags each. But *Sappho*, the later of the two other Coats' boats, though obtaining 4 seconds and 2 thirds, only succeeded in getting a well-earned first on the last day, down Firth, at Largs. Mrs. Peter Simpson, steering her husband's *Helen*, showed some of her pre-war winning form, and looked like staging a come-back by taking 2 firsts on successive days. *Felma* won the Glazebrook Trophy for the best performance over the two Royal Clyde regattas, by just one point, from *Pandora*.

After the very fair turnout of the Eights, and, remembering what a particularly strong class there was here before the war, it will come as a surprise to some readers to learn that there were only two regular Sixes this year. No class on the Clyde has suffered more losses, by death and retirement in the war years, in proportion to its numbers. No less than five owners out of nine or ten have died. Several have dropped out or retired.

One of the first deaths was that of the late J. H. Maurice Clark, whose loss to Clyde racing is not confined to the class in which he happened to race, but to the whole cause of Clyde yachting. I have not the space here in which to refer to all that the name of Maurice Clark meant to the prestige, organization, and encouragement of youngsters in the sport. In future years, as Clyde yachting recovers, and International events return, the gap that he left will be felt even more acutely.

One surprising retirement from active participation in the class was that of J. H. Thom, who put *Circe*, his famous Seawanhaka Cup winner, on the market a few years ago. However, I was pleased to notice that he had not entirely relinquished the tiller, for he was to be seen at the helm of anything from a Dragon to an Eight, on several occasions. And as the master touch was generally quite noticeable in the results, it is understandable that he was a most sought-after guest helmsman.

So there were only two regular starters in the 6-metre class : Ronald Teacher's Nicholson designed *Erica*, and J. Howden Hume's *Johan*, which McGruers had designed and built for the late Donaldson brothers. But what a pair they made ! The daily duels between them made up somewhat for the lack of numbers. Here we had two of the Clyde's best helmsmen pitted against each other, handling the creations of two leading designers and builders. Seldom were they more than a few seconds apart.

I have followed this pair pretty closely throughout the season, but in particular I remember Saturday 6th July, the first of the Royal Northern's two regattas.

We were lying off Kirn, and it was a day of bright sunshine between frequent showers which swept down from the Cowal hills, on a fresh due-westerly. The first leg was a broad reach to the Inverkip mark, and a shower had just passed over, with plenty of wind to speed it on its way.

Ten minutes after the Eights had swept by in tight formation, a cluster of flowing curves and foamy wakes, these two Sixes came bowling along. *Erica* was hot on *Johan's* tail and luffing slightly in the squalls towards her opponent's weather quarter in an endeavour to steal a pocketful of the green boat's wind. She got to within, it seemed, inches of *Johan's* counter, and as they drew abreast I shouted " Step on it," to Alec, my trusty ferryman, and we tried to follow in their lee. But our $7\frac{1}{4}$ knots was not enough to hold these flighty twins. They soon drew away from us as on they went, helter-skelter, yawing and luffing, kicking up their heels in clouds of sea-dust and fighting every inch of it.

Later on, in the same round, we came upon them again, in rather different conditions. They were then off Ashton, running to Rosneath Patch ahead of a big threatening rain squall which was busy blotting out the Firth astern. The weather was now turning the scene back into one like that of the first two days, and even the sails looked grey.

Johan was a minute or two ahead, and her parachute spinnaker, drawing far out beyond her lee bow, was pulling like an impatient kite. However, though the wind was no less, it was interesting to note that in spite of the scudding sail, we were just able to keep up with them.

Later, we turned our attention to *Erica*, whose spinnaker was drawing even better, and looked like recovering a few precious seconds for her. She was on the very fringe of the squall. The wind increased in fierce puffs which, when she rolled, hove her over almost to the rail, and its sudden shifting about in direction gave those on sheet and guy some lively moments to keep control. (How I longed for a blink of sunshine then.) Even Mr. Teacher himself had sometimes to release the tiller for a moment in order to get in that sheet, hand-over-hand.

We followed them to the leeward mark, but it was clearly *Johan's* day again, and she eventually won by just over 4 minutes. *Erica* is a light-weather boat and, as the average strength of wind throughout the Fortnight could hardly be said to favour such, it is perhaps not surprising that *Johan* usually got the better of her and won 7 out of 8 races, though as already said, usually by a matter of seconds.

We dogged these two Sixes with their lovely parachutes until they must have been sick of the sight of the wee white launch. To me those silken shapes, with their infinite variety of flowing curves and translucent shadows, are a continual fascination. Maybe I just have a weakness for them, for my father likens them, in tones of distaste, to " bloated pigs' bellies."

The handicap for the ex-6-metres produced a sufficiently mixed bag to warrant the nickname, " The Cocktail Class." This is the Clyde's nearest equivalent to the Q-class in the South, and it is not solely confined to old Sixes.

This season, the only 30-square-metre, P. H. N. Ulander's *Tarpoon* has turned out regularly. And her Swedish owner has thereby provided further food for argument amongst the theorists on displacement, aspect ratios, overlaps, etc. I would not attempt to draw any conclusions myself, but it was noticeable that the Thirty did not have it all her own way, either on or off the wind, against such well-known boats as *Susette* (Robert Lorimer) and *Vorsa* (Thos. S. Black), on level terms. I even heard it said that she was better than the Sixes on a reach, than in going to windward. In every race but one she was beaten by *Susette*, but she generally got the better of her other opponents, such as *Tystie*—ex-*Saskia II* (Malcolm McGregor), *Suilven* (W. A. Burnet) and *Dubsghe* (H. W. Porter), though she had to allow the latter two 10 secs. per mile.

The turnout in the local Scottish Islands Class O.D.s was disappointing as there were only 4 boats. *Sanda* (Jas. Buchanan), the former class champion, succeeded in saving her reputation by winning 4 firsts and 4 seconds. But *Fidra* (A. R. Keith Thomson) and *Bernera* (Thos. E. Russell) both made her fight hard for it, each having taken a first on two occasions.

Of course, in the now so popular Dragon class we had neither lack of numbers nor lack of good sport. Six visiting boats from Northern Ireland provided that element o keen rivalry that gives such a fillip to the sport, and I am sure the local helmsmen— and helmswomen—must have learned quite a few things from these Irishmen. The growth of this fleet to its peak total of 21 starters on one of the most dismal days has already been mentioned as an indication of this keenness. The principal contest was for the Daly Trophy, which was to be decided on points over the first 8 regattas, all held on the upper-Firth courses. And that all six Irishmen were included in the ten best scores, is some indication of their fine performance.

From the earliest regattas it looked as though the Trophy might soon leave the Clyde. Though the best Clyde boat, and previous holder, *Pinta* (Wm. Russell) had already shown she had lost none of her winning form, the two Irish boats, *Ceres* (W. H. Barnet) and *Portavo* (Sir R. M. T. McConnell) both showed at once that they meant to oust her if possible, " come wind come weather."

Pinta had a bit of bad luck at the Mudhook Y.C.'s opening regatta. Between the prepare and starting guns a fierce squall drove her against the Commodore ship, thus obliging her to retire, and to drop a possible minimum of 12 points for a finish. *Ceres* also dropped 11 points next day by retiring, but she triumphed in spite of this and in the end, led her compatriot, *Portavo*, by 6 points, thus gaining the Trophy. *Pinta* came third, with *Vingthor* (Messrs. McCubbin) fourth, and then the two sister helmswomen, Mrs. Sheila Hinge and Mrs. Molly Mackay in *Argee* and *Lora* respectively.

But it was not only for the prizes that this keen rivalry was evident. One could see them in little bunches fighting it out in small private contests throughout the day, for 7th, 8th or even 15th place.

I remember when the fleet crossed the Firth for the Royal Gourock Y.C.'s day, they had to sail a final " distance " over to Hunter's Quay and back to Ashton to complete the course. It was one of the pleasanter days, with a light-to-moderate S.W. breeze and fitful sunshine. Over at the Hunter's Quay mark boat they made a rather unusual and attractive spectacle as they approached, rounded, and doubled back to the finish in two distinct lanes of traffic, all with a soldier's wind. It was *Pinta's* day, and while she was nearing the finishing line, with *Portavo* about 40 secs. astern, the " also rans " were still coming over to the Hunter's Quay mark in little bunches, fighting it out at close quarters all the way. Meanwhile *Argee*, lying third and slightly in the lead from *Ceres*, was approaching the finishing line which lay obliquely to their course and had to be crossed in the reverse direction. When within a few yards of the line, and Mrs. Hinge seemed to have it " in the bag," *Ceres* by a clever manœuvre nipped round the mark buoy and crossed the line to get the gun 2 seconds ahead.

It is difficult, to appraise the performance of those that raced in the handicap for yachts under 7 tons, as it was only on two occasions that there was any representative turnout. Most had been deterred by the weather on the worst days, others gave up waiting, in despair of its ever improving, whilst one owner I met on the beach on two of the worst days was champing at the bit to start if only another competitor would do likewise.

The last class to start each day (excluding an occasional race for naval whalers) was that of the little Loch Long boats—the smallest of the local one designs. Four or five little 20-ft. sloops turned out on the better days, and *Rhodora* (Messrs. Jeffrey) and *Firefly* (J. Reid, junr.) emerged with honours even, having gained 2 firsts and 1 second flag each.

Altogether it was a memorable Fortnight, notable for its hard-fought contests. The race committees did a good job of work under many difficulties, not least of which was that of obtaining a suitable Commodore vessel each day. This somewhat strained the generosity of owners of the few such boats out this year, and on occasions when a quite small ship had to suffice—and there was a southerly swell with driving rain off Hunter's Quay—conditions were distinctly uncomfortable. I understand it was once suggested, in view of this difficulty, that the Clyde Conference should establish a permanent flagship for the purpose—by fitting out one of Scrutton's barges. However, at Largs, they went one better and chartered the *Boer*, one of the ubiquitous Clyde " puffers." Complete with flags and bunting she carried out her duties at the final regatta as efficiently as any of her more graceful predecessors. Shades of *Para Handy*.

ILLUSTRATIONS ON OPPOSITE PAGE :—

Upper left : Ceres, the Irish Dragon which, with her compatriot *Portavo*, swept the board at the Fortnight.

Upper right : Amita, the most successful boat both in and out of her class, won six firsts in seven starts.

Lower left: Tarpoon, the only 30-square-metre, raced in the ex-six-metre class, and by no means had it all her own way.

Lower right : Sanda, the best boat in the Scottish Islands Class, but she had to concede first place to *Bernetra* and *Fidra* on several occasions.

Top left : Winners of the Prince of Wales Challeng
Cup : Peter Scott and John Winter in *Thunder an
Lightning.*

Top right : *Tuneful* (M. J. Ellison), who had done s
well in the other races during the week, finishe
second.

Centre left : On the reach to the buoy off th
breakwater. Charles Curry in *Thunder* kept we
to windward of E. Bruce Wolfe's *Spider.*

Centre right : *Develin,* sailed by Stewart H. Morri
was the only one of the leaders to carry he
spinnaker to the finishing line.

Lower left : *Hawk, Happy Return* and *Flying Clou
gybing round the leeward mark off Brixha
breakwater.*

The fifty-two boats made a magnificent sight as they crossed the line with a fresh nor'-westerly wind.
Stewart Morris's *Develin*, at the leeward end of the line, led the fleet.

THE PRINCE OF WALES CUP

By B. G. FEARNLEY

(Photographs by the author)

THERE was great activity and excitement at Brixham on Thursday morning 25th July, for that was the day for the first Prince of Wales Cup race since 1939, when Colin Ratsey won it in the American designed *Hawk*.

By the time I arrived in the vicinity of the committee boat there was a seething mass of 52 dinghies sailing here, there and everywhere, all keyed up to the highest pitch, waiting for those last few nerve wracking minutes to pass, before the start. The wind was fresh N.W. and the sun was shining.

As the starting gun boomed out, Stewart Morris's *Develin* came tearing across the leeward end of the line on the starboard tack, with G. V. Lockett's *Trade Wind*, C. R. Martin's *Red Rover*, Sqd. Ldr. C. T. Nance's *Nereid* and J. W. Setchell's *Flying Cloud* close astern. I caught a glimpse of Peter Scott and John Winter in *Thunder and Lightning* on the port tack before they were lost to view in the mass of boats.

Stewart Morris led the fleet for some way, increasing his lead slightly, but on going about on to the port tack he had to give way to two boats and so lost the lead to W. Noel Jordan and Beecher Moore in *Indigo*. The positions of the leaders were now changed to *Indigo*, *Elan*, *Develin*, Roy Dann's *Nimrod* and Tom Thornycroft in *Gyrinus*. At the first mark *Indigo*, pointing very high, had opened out quite a useful lead, and on the reach out to the next mark off the breakwater at Brixham she increased it considerably, leaving the next half-dozen boats to fight it out in a close bunch. Bruce Wolfe in *Spider* planed past C. H. Chichester-Smith's *Mirage* and Michael Ellison's *Tuneful*. Places were constantly changing : *Thunder and Lightning* sailed through *Elan's* lee into third place while *Tuneful*, planing very fast, passed *Mirage*.

Rounding the second mark the positions had changed to *Indigo*, *Joyful*, *Thunder and Lightning*, *Windstar*, *Develin*, *Elan*, *Tuneful*, *Spider* and *Archangel*.

On this run *Indigo's* lead had been shortened and on turning the mark to commence the second round she was only three seconds ahead of *Joyful* and twenty ahead of

155

Thunder and Lightning, but with John Winter at the helm, *Thunder and Lightning* out-pointed *Indigo* and on reaching the weather mark was eleven seconds ahead, with *Joyful* now in third place thirty-five seconds behind. *Nereid* hit the mark and retired.

At the Brixham mark the boats were all very closely bunched, the first four places being unchanged, but fifth and sixth were *Develin* and *Windstar* respectively ; in gybing round the mark they both lost some ground to the leaders. *Spider* was the first to set her spinnaker, but was quickly followed by *Thunder* and Lt.-Col. R. H. Farrant's *Fearless ;* however, it seemed very doubtful if spinnakers would pay as the wind had veered more abeam than in the previous round.

Thunder and Lightning had by then developed quite a good lead, being one minute eleven seconds ahead of *Tuneful*, the second boat, and one minute thirty seconds ahead of *Indigo* with *Joyful* and *Develin* fourth and fifth. Peter Scott took the helm for the beat at the commencement of the third round and increased his lead by thirty-five seconds from the second boat. *Indigo*, having been passed by *Windstar*, *Thunder* and *Develin* was now lying sixth. Having gybed round the Brixham mark at the end of the reach, *Indigo*, *Spider* and *Elan* all set spinnakers.

The positions of the first five were unchanged as they turned the mark to start the fourth round. Shortly after rounding the mark at the end of the beat, John Winter again took the helm and, increasing his lead, was one minute fifty-eight seconds ahead of *Tuneful* at the completion of the round, with *Thunder*, *Joyful*, *Windstar* and *Develin* strung out behind.

At the start of the fifth and last round Peter Scott relieved John Winter at the helm for the beat, but on finishing that they changed back again, and with a lead of about half a mile from *Tuneful* they gybed round the mark for the final run home.

It was rather a procession over the finishing line, with Peter Scott and John Winter two minutes twenty-six seconds ahead of *Tuneful*, and with *Thunder*, *Joyful*, *Develin* and *Spider* one behind the other. Stewart Morris was the only one of the leaders to carry his spinnaker to the end.

On the reach out to the leeward mark off the breakwater at Brixham. Charles Curry's *Thunder* in the foreground.

A CORNISH VENTURE

By ERIC C. HISCOCK

OUR plans for our first real cruise together in our own little ship were ambitious ones, for it was only during the war that I had acquired Susan, my wife and permanent crew, and as I had previously been a single-hander, I imagined that with a crew all things would be possible. Cruising on paper is a delightful occupation; there is no violent motion to make one sick, no head-winds against which to battle, and one can cover the most surprising distances without the slightest trouble. So we, having spread out the charts on the living-room floor, decided that when we left the Solent, Helford in Cornwall would be our first port of call. We would then slip round Land's End when the god of the weather was not looking, and within a week we ought to be in Scotland.

Captain Lecky must have been a very wise man, and his little rhyme about the weather had always appeared to me to be very sound. It runs :—

Dirty days hath September,
April, June, and November.
From January up to May
The rain it raineth every day.
All the rest have thirty-one
Without a blessed gleam of sun :
And if any of them had two and thirty,
They'd be just as wet and twice as dirty.

No doubt he included fog under the general heading of " dirty," but he seems to have made no mention of calms, and on our little trip we suffered a good deal from both these things. So I had better tell you at once that we never succeeded in rounding Land's End after all. For this the weather was mainly responsible, but the fact that our holiday was eventually reduced to a bare fortnight, had something to do with it.

In times so lean as these, it was with a car surprisingly well filled with provisions that we arrived at the old quay by Gins Farm on the bank of the Beaulieu River. But, taking advantage of the arrangements made for provisioning yachts for a period of a fortnight or more, we had filled in the necessary forms at the Southampton custom house, and Mr. Buckle of St. Michael's Square had done the rest. There were many tins of fruit, jam, vegetables and meat ; there were eggs, bread, butter and bacon ; there was even a bottle of whisky. Mr. Buckle appears to understand most thoroughly yachtsmen and their needs.

The stowage of all these things in addition to charts, clothes, photographic equipment, a typewriter, and all the other miscellaneous items for which we thought we might find a need while cruising, was something of a problem in a 4-tonner, and as we are very poor, that is the largest vessel Susan and I can afford to own. But *Wanderer II* has good locker accommodation. In this, and in most other respects, she suits us very well ; we have confidence in her because she has carried me in safety, if in no great comfort, some 10,000 miles ; she has roomy decks, for her cabin-top is narrow ; she can carry her own 7-foot dinghy, and her insides are, in our opinion, more convenient than those of many other vessels in which we have sailed. But our tastes in accommodation are simple : all we ask are comfortable berths on which to sleep, locker space for everything so that no stowing of loose articles is needed before putting to sea, a galley in which it is possible to cook a meal when under way, and an open coal fireplace to keep us warm and dry all the wet gear.

These requirements *Wanderer* fulfills to our satisfaction. Her rig, that of a gaff cutter with a large topsail and plenty of light weather canvas, appeals to our æsthetic tastes and gets us along very well in most kinds of weather. In a short popple of sea she will not go to windward, but very few vessels measuring only 20 feet 9 inches on the waterline will do so either. Her beam is just over 7 feet and she draws 5 feet of water. We have not got an engine because our water tank occupies the space that one would need ; also, we get a certain satisfaction and an added spice of excitement from cruising under sail alone. There are many hazards which have to be avoided : the tide may be setting, or will soon be setting one towards some shoal or rocky patch, and without a responsive engine beneath the cockpit floor, one has to jockey for position so as to be in the correct place at the right time. It is true that on occasions a harbour cannot be entered because the wind is contrary and the tide against one ; but if it is possible to get in, the satisfaction of doing so under sail alone is very great. However, the days of sail are almost over, and I suppose that if ever we are rich enough to have another yacht, she will possess an engine ; we will then get further afield in a limited time with far less effort and worry, but I sometimes wonder whether we shall get quite the same pleasure from our cruising.

At six o'clock the next morning we were under way with a fair tide and a light N. wind. With topsail, and yankee jib-topsail (a fine big sail extending from the bowsprit end to the mast-head) drawing well, we slipped down the calm Solent and out through the Needles Channel. Off the Bridge buoy we set the patent log and a course W. by S.¼S. for a point five miles off Portland Bill ; having once been set into the race when attempting to pass inside it without an engine, I now always pass that dangerous place almost out of sight of land. But by noon we were quite becalmed south of Anvil Point ; the tide was against us, and as we were starting to lose ground, we anchored with the kedge and warp in fifteen fathoms.

There we lay quite peacefully until the evening turn of the tide, when a light breeze from the west sprang up. We made one short tack close in under St. Alban's Head, across the tiered ridges of which the slanting sunlight was casting curious lines of shadow, so that the valley beside it looked like a vast ampitheatre ready set for some gigantic audience. Then we stood offshore, and with the wind freeing a little, we were five miles off the sinister, wedge-shaped peninsula of Portland by midnight. There we remained utterly becalmed in the steamer track for several hours, but oddly enough we did not lose much ground, though the tide should have been setting to the eastward once more. Presently a fine N. wind came to rustle us across West Bay.

Dawn brought with it some fog patches as the night wind slowly died away and left us stationary, but every now and then we got a glimpse of Start Point and the high land behind Dartmouth. We breakfasted leisurely and with comfort, trimmed and filled the navigation lamps and had generally got the ship tidied up before the wind came again. As the tide by then was foul and the wind was dead ahead, there seemed little prospect of being able to beat round the Start against it, so we sailed into Start Bay and anchored near its southern end in ten fathoms off Hallsands,

Wanderer II, the author's 4-ton cutter, carries her dinghy on deck amidships.

there to wait for the fair tide which was due to begin about tea time. But just as we were preparing to leave, the siren at the lighthouse started to give out each minute, its mournful blast. The whole great roadstead in which we lay still gleamed in the afternoon sunlight ; the golden beaches of Hall- Bee- and Slaptonsands stood out brilliantly below the red and green patchwork pattern of the rich Devon countryside. But billowing over the cockscomb of the point, swirling round the high thin masts of the radar station, and in places creeping stealthily down to the sea on the near side, was a bank of thick white fog. While we in the bay still basked in hot sunshine, Start Point played hide-and-seek in his cottonwool eiderdown, a game we watched impatiently, for a fair tide was running to waste. But at five p.m. the fog bank rolled out to sea, we got our anchor and with a whole sail breeze from the west, rounded the corner and beat on down the coast past Prawle Point against a short, steep and most uncomfortable little sea.

Coming down Channel, Susan had once or twice been seasick, but she had her own peculiar ideas on the cure of that malady. Her method was to prepare hot meals at frequent intervals *and* eat them. So feeling a little squeamish as we bounced about off Salcombe, she at once went below and set about preparing a most appetizing stew. We were in the midst of eating this when away to windward we spied another bank of fog rapidly advancing on us, and from it came the sad hooting of steamers.

The anchorage in Helford River, with Abraham's Bosom in the background.

Considering that was not an ideal place in which to remian fog-bound, we bore away for Salcombe which was close under our lee, and just managed to reach South Sand Bay, the first possible anchorage inside the bar, when the fog descended on us from the heights of Bolt Head, blotting out everything. Even the sandy beach, close to which we lay at anchor, was at times almost invisible. We were glad to be in out of it, and enjoyed a peaceful night, except for some rolling during the ebb, which is a peculiarity of Salcombe, and can only be avoided with certainty by going right up into the Bag beyond the town.

The fog persisted until we had breakfasted the following morning, but then cleared in rather a half-hearted sort of way, and plagued with fierce little squalls and calms, we took more than an hour to reach the open water less than a mile away. With a light head-wind and an uncomfortable little sea, we pitched and banged about, and only with the greatest difficulty succeeded in passing Bolt Tail, for the fair tide had finished long before we reached it. But beyond, in Bigbury Bay, the tide was very slack, and as the day improved from a grey dreariness to a bright sparkle, we enjoyed ourselves and made slightly better progress.

Off Revelstoke Point the wind suddenly veered to N.W. by W., so we went about and at supper time passed south of the Eddystone lighthouse. There the wind backed again, and for a while we considered whether we would put into Cawsand Bay for the night, for we were getting rather tired of our slow progress ; but the glass had been dropping slowly and steadily all day, and although the evening was fine and clear, a solar halo and thin streamers of cirrus suggested that there was more wind to come ; so we thought it best to get on to the westward while that was still possible.

At nine p.m. the Eddystone bore E. by N., three miles distant, and we went about. At midnight we tacked again off Looe where the bright lights of the fishing fleet were dancing all around. Once again we were becalmed for some hours, but shortly before dawn the wind came again, freshening and backing, so that very soon we were able to head clear of the Dodman on the port tack, and a little later sailed with a free wind and eased sheets. Rapidly our speed improved until we were logging over five knots as we swept past that bold headland in the grey light of the overcast dawn ; the yankee sheet was hard and rigid, the backstay vibrating with the strain. Veryan and Gerrans Bays were soon astern ; Falmouth Harbour opened to the north of us, and was as quickly shut in again as we slipped into the smooth waters of Helford River, where we brought up in the anchorage above the bar at breakfast time.

At noon heavy rain set in, and for the next two days the bad weather which the glass had foretold enveloped us ; strong winds from S. and W. ruffled the anchorage, and conditions were not encouraging for the rounding of the Lizard and Land's End. But although delays are irksome when time is limited, and the large mail which we had received indicated that we could not afford to be away for more than a fortnight, we much prefer to be weatherbound at Helford than anywhere else. It is one of the jolliest anchorages on the South Coast, and we have some very good friends there. Also, we were delighted to meet Dr. and Mrs. Pye in *Moonraker*, a Polperro fishing boat of about 10-tons, which they had bought and converted most successfully to their own ideas of what a comfortable cruiser ought to be. They were bound for Eire, and we hoped to sail in company with them as far as Land's End, where our courses would separate.

The third morning at Helford dawned fine and sunny, and at seven a.m. *Moonraker* and *Wanderer* left the river together. Both were carrying tanned working canvas and topsails, and must have made a most attractive picture as they slipped quietly out in the early morning sunshine. An hour later the Manacles buoy was abeam ; the wind was west, moderate for the most part, but fresh at times. On the starboard tack we made slow progress against a lumpy sea, but the tide was with us, and at eleven a.m., when the Lizard Lighthouse bore N. three miles, we went about. The sea was certainly not heavy, but it was steep and sudden, and sometimes piled on top of the rounded Atlantic swell ; no doubt it was disturbed by the weather-going tide. Though Susan had by then quite cured herself of seasickness, we both felt giddy and light headed at times. McMullen in his classic *Down Channel* mentions this same peculiarity of the seas off the Lizard. I quote from his cruise of the *Leo* : ". . . . neither the boy nor myself could look outside the boat after the first few minutes without turning giddy. . . . I felt, besides, the wretched weakening sensation in the spine which most people feel when tossed in a high swing against their will."

But after passing the Head the seas became easier, and we were able once more to take an interest in our consort. When first we had begun turning to windward, *Moonraker*, as was to be expected of a larger ship, sailed much faster than *Wanderer*, but she did not appear to lie so close to the wind. This was more evident when she came about, for instead of passing well ahead, she crossed tacks with us at quite close quarters. In the conditions then prevailing, the two boats were very evenly matched, which is just as it should be when sailing in company, and we got much comfort and pleasure at *Moonraker's* proximity.

With the Lizard astern both yachts were on the port tack, but our friends appeared to sag away considerably, and presently we lost sight of them in Mounts Bay, for visibility was indifferent. At three p.m. we closed with the land in the neighbourhood of Lamorna Cove, which was looking very grand in the sunshine, and went about. But the fair tide was done, the wind was increasing so that the topsail had to come in, and when, having stood out to sea for two hours, we went about and again closed

L

with the land, we found that progress had been very poor. Instead of weathering the Runnelstone, as we had expected to do, we were considerably to leeward of it.

Only then did the shortness of our holiday impress itself upon us, and we argued that as already half of it had passed, to continue for Scotland would be quite absurd ; even the Isles of Scilly, some twenty-seven miles to windward, seemed out of reach for the moment. But I never am at my best as night draws on, the wind increases, the sea rises and the glass begins to fall, so it was with only slight reluctance that we bore away for Mounts Bay and Newlyn.

Dusk was upon us as we approached the harbour, and for a little while we could not distinguish its grey breakwaters from the indistinct grey background of the shore. But then the south pier light began to flash, and as we headed for it a faint cry of " Wanderer-r-r-r " reached us. This, we soon discovered, came from Pye who, with his crew all sick, had wisely entered Newlyn in the afternoon. He had been watching us and feared we might be going to Penzance.

I was a little concerned as to how to enter the place without an engine, for the entrance is too narrow for windward work. But, as so often happens at dusk, the wind in the the lee of the land dropped completely for a little while ; with the sweep over the stern we were able to scull the yacht in, and without the slightest difficulty moored alongside *Moonraker*.

With the lamps along the quay only partly illuminating the hulls and spars of the fishing fleet, with the occasional mutter of a boat's engine and the soft Cornish voices of her crew, Newlyn seemed a most romantic place in the stillness of the evening.

But in the morning all had changed. Low grey clouds drove across the sky from the south-west, the wind hummed a deep note in the rigging, and dark catspaws hurried across the green water of the harbour. *Moonraker* was going to the Scillies, and Pye suggested that we should go there too, but I would decide on nothing until I had seen what conditions were like outside, and I had been depressed a little by a fisherman who said we would both be back in half an hour.

At nine-fifteen a.m., still lashed alongside one another, *Moonrakers'* engine took us both neatly out of the harbour, for which I was very thankful, as we would indeed have been hard put to it to leave our restricted berth onto which the wind was blowing, under sail. But remaining alongside during this manoeuvre was a mistake, for the moment we had cleared the pier-heads we came into a slight swell which was setting into the bay, and before we could cast off, and in spite of fenders, *Moonraker's* port chain-plates had ripped off a foot of our teak rail. Quickly the lines were let go, and making sail, we lay close-hauled on the starboard tack heading about S. by E.

That day there was a heavier sea and more wind, so that even under lower sail and second jib *Wanderer* was hard pressed, while *Moonraker*, better able to stand up to her canvas, made good weather of it, and an hour later tacked and stood across our bows well ahead. Susan and I decided that the Scillies were quite out of the question, and that in the circumstances we would be better employed from a journalistic point of view to the eastward of the Lizard. So we continued on our way close-hauled and hoped that we would manage to make a sufficient offing, for the seas were steep and we were making considerable leeway.

The last we saw of sturdy little *Moonraker*, her black hull glistening with wet, her brown sails bellied out in firm and powerful curves, she was heading about W. by

N., and with a fair tide under her we hoped she would have a good passage. She was soon lost to our view in the general murk.

Wanderer meanwhile was driving along under what was rapidly becoming a press of sail as the wind freshened, but I knew she would need driving if we were to get the offing that we needed before the tide turned to sweep us into the race off the Lizard. Time and again she buried her lee deck right up to the cabin-top, and occasionally a bucketfull or two of water would dash in over the cockpit coaming. Heavy deluges of spray drove with a hiss up over the weather rail and rattled into the sails ; the main-sail was soon soaked right up to the crosstrees. But all the while she made steady progress, and the sinister grey line of the shore under her lee got no closer. In fact she was doing well enough for such a little vessel. Below decks everything was in good shape, but to move about down there was very difficult, not only on account of the motion, which was violent in the extreme, but because of the great angle of heel ; the cabin lamp was canted so far over that its globe was pressed hard against the outer ring of the gimballs, and later when we tried it like that at anchor, the angle, considerably greater than forty-five degrees, seemed quite an impossible one.

Our anxiety about weathering the Lizard race soon vanished, and I believe we cleared the Head by between six and eight miles, but in poor visibility it is difficult to judge distances.

When we considered that a sufficient offing had been obtained, we bore away, and life at once became more reasonable. We even managed to get something to eat. But although we were no longer torn at by the wind and deluged with driving spray, the helmsman's job became much more difficult and responsible. In order to keep well clear of the race, which would have been dangerous in such conditions even with a lee-going tide, we could not run dead before the wind, for such a course, N.E., would have closed with the land too rapidly. Instead we kept the wind as much as possible on the starboard quarter, bearing away dead before it only when a particularly steep and threatening sea compelled us to do so for the safety of the vessel.

The Lizard lighthouse bore N. at three p.m., and there was then a heavy sea running. No doubt steering would have been easier under reduced sail, but Wanderer leaves a very clean wake and can continue to run at speed with safety when a more beamy vessel, or one with heavier quarters, might interfere with the seas astern and cause them to break. But even so it was noticable at times that the seas immediately astern and towering above us, were steeper than those elsewhere, and were capped with hungry, foaming crests. It was at such moments that I felt it imperative to put the yacht's stern to them. Susan, standing chocked-off in the companionway, told me afterwards that sometimes she had to look away, for it seemed to her that the sea astern really was going to overwhelm us. Sometimes a louder roar than usual from aft compelled me to look round, and I did not care for what I saw. On other occasions, as a foaming crest passed beneath us, for a moment the tiller felt light and useless in my hand. Those, and those only, were the danger moments when the greatest care was needed ; for at other times careless steering simply brought a just, and wet, reward. If I ignored a steep sea and let Wanderer take it on the quarter, a bit of the crest would explode against the weather side just abreast of the rigging ; then a fountain of water would leap up into the air, wait for Wanderer to carry me beneath it, and then fall on my head to stream down my neck and pour out of my trouser legs. Fortunately it was warm.

Now, as I have said, to continue running with safety it was necessary to bear away dead before the more threatening seas, but an unthought-of hazard suddenly reared itself up out of the murk on our lee quarter—a steamer. I believe that she, seeing a tiny white yacht fleeing up Channel with water spouting from her scuppers, thought we were in difficulties. She came on at speed until she lay close under our lee bow, in exactly the position to which I wished to point each time I needed to bear away, and there she slowed down. She was much too close for comfort, and if she persisted in holding her position, I would no longer be able to continue bearing away when necessary, or so I thought. Near though she was, the ship was frequently quite hidden from our view by an intervening sea ; even her mast-heads vanished ; but of course it does not need a very large sea to hide one vessel from another when both happen to be in the trough at the same time.

We had no means of asking her to move out of the way, and I feared that any gesticulations on our part might give the false impression that we required assistance ; so, asking Susan for a dry box of matches, ostentatiously I filled and lit my pipe. But I was becoming almost desperate before the people in that ship appreciated that we were not making such bad weather of it after all, and thankfully I saw her increase speed and draw ahead.

When we had passed the Lizard the seas grew easier. We ran on an E.N.E. course until it was reckoned we could fetch the Manacles on the other gybe, then gybed, and in smooth water at five p.m. had the Manacles buoy abeam. There we altered course for Falmouth, and with the wind almost abeam, I realised at last how hard it was blowing. We simply stormed along and covered the five and a half miles from the buoy to the Black Rock beacon in just under fifty minutes, a speed of something more than six knots. We were soon snugly at anchor in Falmouth off the Royal Cornwall Y.C., little the worse for our heavy going. But *Wanderer* had apparently taken a dislike to a book I had recently written ; carefully arranging a deck leak over the one copy of it which was on board, she had converted it most thoroughly into the original pulp from which it had sprung ; no other book in the shelf had been harmed in any way.

The wind took off in the night, and the following afternoon, when we set out for Fowey, was only blowing with moderate force from the west, but the weather god had other pleasantries in store for us. No sooner had we left St. Anthony astern than visibility grew poor and a compass course for the Dodman became necessary : shortly after we were enveloped in real fog. Judging by the blurred nature of the horizon—and there was nothing else to look at—I think our own small circle of visibility seldom had a radius of as much as a quarter of a mile. I considered it more prudent to continue for the Dodman than to try to beat back for Falmouth, so as Susan is much more conscientious at the helm than I am, she steered a careful compass course while I played with the chart and the book of tidal streams in an attempt to estimate the time of our arrival at the Dodman. Fortunately that headland is steep-to, and I deemed it safe to approach within a hundred yards or so of it, but if by chance we missed it, I was determined to stand out to sea until such time as the weather might clear.

As the zero hour of five fifteen approached, I went on deck and peered ahead and to port, anxiously looking for a darkening of the white blanket. As we slipped along, so our own small isolated little world of nothing seemed to slide along with us. Always it was there : our vision-bounding wall of vapour. And then, quite suddenly, while I was looking the other way, Susan said she thought she saw a darkening of it. I turned, and there below the faint grey smudge appeared the white gleam of breakers a couple of hundred yards away under our lee. Only a few feet of the cliffs behind them were visible ; higher up everything was shrouded in impenetrable fog. But this I knew to be the Dodman, and when the coast receded to the N.E. we altered course and followed it. The wind, there drawing up along the land, was S.W., and there was a curiously lumpy sea as though the wind and tide were opposed, which, in fact, they were not. But for the moment our troubles were over ; the fog was lifting, and by the time we had Chapel Point abeam, visibility had improved to over a mile. So we boldly altered course for Gribbin Head, on the last hop to Fowey, at which port we had an idea we might meet our friends the Webbs in *Eudoia* who had left the Solent a day after us. But we had barely covered a mile on our way when the fog closed down again as thick as ever. Once again we went through all the worry of a foggy landfall, but this time we had an additional anxiety, for off Gribbin Head lies the Cannis Rock which is covered at three-quarters flood. But the distance was only five miles, and I thought we ought to be able to make the Cannis buoy with certainty. So we held on, and in time had again the satisfaction of making another successful landfall. The fog was thicker than ever as we approached Fowey, but with the aid of the compass and occasional glimpses of the more prominent pieces of the coast, we were able to find our way in without difficulty, and keeping to the western side, seeing nothing of the eastern entrance point, we came-to off the town just above *Eudoia*.

The entrance and outer harbour, Mevagissey.

Above : Goran Haven.   *Below* : The fishing fleet in the inner harbour, Mevagissey.

The fog lasted in all three days, and during that time life on board was clammy. All our belongings became damp and sticky, mildew grew with surprising rapidity, particularly on the bread, the idle halyards shrunk so much that some of them would no longer reach their pins, and yet it was too hot and stuffy to allow us to light our coal fire and pretend that winter was upon us.

But in time the sun struggled through the mist and quickly gobbled up the remnants of it. On a day of real high summer without a single cloud, we hoisted all our summer finery and beat most pleasantly over a sea of indescribably brilliant blue, back towards the Dodman. We had just one more day to spare before hurrying on to the Solent, and as we felt quite certain of having a fair wind for that passage, we decided to spend our last night in the Cornish fishing harbour of Mevagissey. Some of the fascination of that place we had gleaned from the chart which showed a small walled enclosure in a cleft of the cliffs, an enclosure in which it would be possible to lie afloat if sufficient room could be found.

But first we went to Goran Haven, a tiny fishing village which lies in the corner of a sandy bay on the east side of the Dodman. The chart told us little of this place except that the bay was practically free from dangers, and the *Channel Pilot* mentioned in passing that there were the remains of a breakwater there. But no chart was necessary as we beat into that brilliant bay, for the sea was so clear that weed patches and rocks on the bottom were quite distinct, and we were able to select a sandy spot on which to drop our anchor. Then, launching the dinghy, we rowed ashore and landed on the beach inside the breakwater which, far from being a ruin, we discovered to be in excellent repair ; a solid, well built stone structure harbouring within its short protecting arm a dozen or more small fishing boats which dried out at low water.

The village consisted of a few steep and twisted narrow streets thronged with a huddled gathering of small stone cottages tightly packed as though for mutual protection. The place had none of the trippery vulgarity which in these days of motoring has come to violate the better known examples of Cornish architecture such as Polperro.

As we strolled round the village, we wondered who had built it and why. An agricultural village one can easily understand, for the landowners had the cottages built to house their workpeople. But a fisherman, in the days when Goran Haven was built, worked only for himself, and presumably must have quarried the stone and built his own house. Perhaps that accounts for the most refreshing lack of planning which is evident in such places. But it must have been a vast undertaking for amateur stone masons to build such a massive breakwater, if indeed they did build it. And in the days before refrigeration and efficient transport, who, we wondered bought, and ate the fish on the proceeds of which the whole community depended ?

In the evening we went aboard again and with a failing wind sailed quietly round to Mevagissey. Slipping in between the outstretched grey stone walls of the harbour, our noses were assailed by an almost overpowering smell of fish. It was not an unpleasant smell, as smells go, but it was startling in its pungency. There was a loud crying from a great gathering of gulls ; every possible point of vantage, every chimney pot and gable of the village, every boat and mast and seat and wall and bollard had its gull, while the air was filled with their flashing white underbodies and outspread wings, as they soared and wheeled and fought for the delectable bits of offal thrown out from the moored fishing boats whose crews were cleaning the day's catch.

Because of this great clamorous colony, the place was wonderfully clean ; no unpleasant traces of its industry were visible in the harbour, and the water was so clean that we were able to watch our anchor plunge to the bottom in a clear space between the mooring chains of the fishing boats.

We brought up just within the entrance on the starboard hand, where we lay in eight feet of water at low tide, well out of the fairway to the inner harbour along which there was a constant coming and going of boats ; many of them were open, but the larger ones were decked, and had a fish-hold and a tiny wheelhouse.

Mevagissey was fascinating. The fishing season was in full swing ; there were boxes laid out in rows on the quay ready for the catch from the incoming boats, and motor lorries waiting there to take it all away. Everyone seemed busy and interested in his job, and we were pleased to see so many young men engaged in the industry. The larger boats had crews of three or four, and in many cases the oldest member could not have been more than twenty-five years old.

There in that narrow valley between the cliffs was a self contained community living, and apparently thriving in a quiet and unostentatious manner, entirely on its own efforts. We saw only one pub ', which was closed for lack of beer, and several chapels. Cigarettes were unobtainable, and most of the village cooking appeared to be done by the local baker : on a large table in his shop we saw many dinner-laden pie-dishes ready waiting to be slipped into the oven as soon as the bread had been baked. Some of the cottages were squalid, and many of them lacked a garden or even a back yard, so that the weekly wash had to be hung on lines across the pavementless streets. But the people had a contented look about them and an air as though to say : " Our job is fish, and we're busy fishing."

At noon on the following day, and with all sail including the yankee set to light variable airs, we slipped out of the little harbour homeward bound. We took with us in our cabin a lingering aroma of fish, as though some freshly caught mackerel had just been fried on the galley stove ; and long after the shore had receded into the distance, our ears still rang with the wild clamour of the Mevagissey gulls.

In the late afternoon we decided to have a look at Polperro, as it was not far off our course, and to sail into its tiny harbour if that were possible. But as we approached the little cleft in which the harbour lies, the wind blew with some strength directly out of it, and as we considered the channel too narrow to beat into, we continued on our way to Rame Head.

Of course we ought to have made full use of that fair wind to carry us on up Channel, but as we were anxious to have a look at Cawsand, there seemed no reason why we should not spend a comfortable night there at anchor and continue in daylight. So we beat up into the bay and came-to off the very attractive village, in three fathoms at dusk.

That is the sort of mistake which I so frequently make. It is only with the greatest effort that I ever manage to tear myself away from the West Country at all, and even then I always have to make just one more stop, forgetting the golden rule for successful

Illustrations on opposite page :—

Top : The village of Cawsand from the anchorage.
Centre : Bolt Tail on the South Devon coast.
Lower : The Island landfall. The Needles lighthouse and Sun Corner from the westward.

passage-making : never waste a fair wind, for sooner or later it will come ahead, and that is the time for dallying.

All night the fair wind blew to waste, and in the morning the last breath of it took us into the gunnery range which exists to the eastward of Plymouth. We were almost becalmed there when a high speed launch towing a target came tearing out of the Sound, and firing commenced. To our consternation we saw that the shots were all falling between us and the shore : that is a very different thing from being fired over by large guns, and struck us as most unsafe. Presently another launch came out and asked us quite politely to go away. We tried to sail to the westward, but with very little success as we barely had steerage way, but when the navy ceased fire to drink its mid-day tot, we took the opportunity of a fair tide to sneak across the range, and were well clear the other side of it when the guns opened fire again.

With light fluky airs mostly from ahead, we drifted and sailed across Bigbury Bay towards Bolt Tail, by which time the east going stream was slacking ; but we made the best use we could of the last of it by sculling, taking ten minute spells each. Off Bolt Head, however, the tide was definitely adverse, and only with the greatest difficulty did we manage to squeeze round the corner, where the tide was setting us towards the Mewstone, and anchored in the south end of Starhole Bay, almost exhausted by our efforts. We had not wished to bring up in that bay at all, for we knew that its bottom must be foul with all that remained of the ill fated *Herzogen Cecille* ; but the tide forbade us reaching any other place.

Night was upon us by the time the sails were stowed and everything had been got ready for a quick departure should the wind come on-shore. The sea was calm, but there was sufficient ground-swell to set up a mournful sobbing and sucking along the rocky shore, as though the sea was lamenting its cruelty to the fine barque whose bones lay there below. The jagged mass of Bolt Head loomed above us, its shadow turning the sea to ink, so that although the shore line could not be defined, we appeared to be anchored much too close to it. An angry red afterglow from the setting sun gave the evening a threatening appearance, and even the cries of the gulls seemed hushed.

We slept uneasily, and when at three a.m. a faint air came in from the N.E., we decided to leave that eerie place without delay. But by the time we had set full sail and shortened in the chain, the air had died away ; but we determined to leave just the same. Because we feared what the tide might do with us once we had left the slack water of the bay, we launched the dinghy, and with Susan towing in her while I stood aft sculling with the sweep, we managed to get clear without being set down onto the Mewstone. We continued this method of propulsion along the coast, past Prawle Point and on towards Lannacombe Bay where we intended to wait for a wind. But before we reached an anchorage there, a breeze came from N.E. again, so that we were able to begin sailing, and with a favourable tide beneath us, we got well clear of Start Point before the next calm, in which we took the dinghy aboard.

Light airs, calms and brilliant sunshine were our lot throughout that day, and I do not know how *Wanderer* accomplished it, but by six o'clock in the evening she had brought Portland into sight. But all that night we lay utterly becalmed, so that by dawn the land had not changed its bearing appreciably. It lay there faint with distance and early morning haze, and then disappeared completely in the mist. Warmer and warmer grew the decks in the direct rays of the sun which the mist did nothing to temper, until they were too hot for our bare feet. Though we frequently splashed bucketfulls of water on them, they were dry again almost before the last trickle had run from the scuppers. The gaff jaws creaked, and the reef points pattered against the mainsail as we rolled gently in the oily swell which reflected the glare from the pale blue sky above.

Our bread had become so stale inside its mouldy crusts as to be almost inedible, but when we tried to toast it, the heat from the toaster, which had almost burnt through and would long since have been replaced if such things were obtainable today, made life below intolerable ; so we ate ship's biscuits instead. Nothing among our tinned provisions appealed to our jaded palates which craved for a crisp salad, fresh fruit and a tall iced drink, but all we could raise in that line were tomatoes and tepid lime juice. Even for those things we could raise no appetite until we had plunged overboard into the calm chill water and refreshed ourselves with a fish's eye view of our little floating home. To add to our feeling of depression the close air throbbed all day long with the reverberating boom of distant gunfire.

From time to time faint airs came to touch us and give steerage way for a little while, but none of them came to stay, so it was not until six o'clock that evening, just twenty-four hours after we had first sighted it, that Portland Bill, appearing through the mist again, bore north. And then at last a light breeze came to put our sails gently to sleep, the stem chuckled musically as it parted the water, and little bubbles slipped hissing along our sides.

We never saw the Shambles light vessel that evening, and except for the Bill, the coast was shrouded in mist ; but a fine fair tide hurried us along in company with many hundreds of pit-props which were drifting about in the Channel at that time, and when it had finished at ten-thirty p.m., we anchored in twenty fathoms with the kedge and warp, hung the riding light in the rigging, and turned in with the intention of looking out every half hour or so to see that all was well.

But we both slept like the dead until six o'clock next morning, when we woke to another day of calm and blazing sunshine ; for the moment visibility had improved, and we found ourselves about four miles south of St. Albans Head. As *Wanderer* had already swung to the first of the flood, we got the anchor aboard and drifted on. But as the power of the sun increased, the heat haze obscured the land and the horizon once more.

When, according to my reckoning, the tide should have done, we anchored again, but no sooner had the hook reached the bottom that it was evident that the tide was still setting to the east. So we got the thing up and drifted for another hour before letting go again, that time to find that the tide really had turned.

From our anchorage we could see nothing, and I was a little anxious, for I believed we were well south of the latitude of the Needles, and if that were so, the next flood would carry us along south of the Isle of Wight instead of through the Needles Channel, which was where we wished to go.

But at noon a W.S.W. breeze sprang up. We weighed the anchor, thus completing a total of a hundred fathoms of warp hauled in that day, and with the large spinnaker set in an enormous bag from the bowsprit end, headed north in order to jockey for a better tidal position. Shortly afterwards, although the Needles were still invisible, the high land above them could be made out. All through the afternoon we played at shifting sails to take every advantage of the light and variable airs, and a dozen times or more we must have gybed and re-set the spinnaker the other side if it did not require to be set from the bowsprit end, and about tea time we slipped into the Needles Channel.

With the tide gathering momentum beneath us, we were hurried along up past the Elbow buoy, the Warden and the N.E. Shingles, and an hour later were spilt out of the tidal whirls in Hurst Narrows onto the still and muddy waters of the Solent.

More quietly now, but still with a strong fair tide, and with the gear no longer creaking and slamming in the swell, we ghosted on past the low New Forest shore, up past the Needs Oar cottages to Lepe, and so into the Beaulieu River. There the yankee took the place of the spinnaker which had served us well that day, and in short tacks we beat slowly on between the reed-fringed banks of the placid river with a slowly dying breeze, and the sun had set as we let go our anchor in the old familiar place off Gins Farm.

We had made good a distance of 434 miles, but in the longest calm I ever remember had taken nearly four and a half days to cover the last 150 of them.

INDEX TO ADVERTISERS

A new
C.I. (Diesel Oil) MARINE ENGINE
for a wide range of craft—

—the
THORNYCROFT
SIX-CYLINDER, TYPE RTR.6
55/65 b.h.p. ENGINE

Features of
OUTSTANDING VALUE
to commercial and private users :

Small overall size and weight; Economy in operation ; Really quiet running ; No fire risk ; Cooling by closed circuit or sea water ; Available with direct drive or water-cooled 2 to 1 reducing gear ; Low-priced quickly-acquired spares, due to large engine production.

OTHER TYPES AVAILABLE:
PETROL/PARAFFIN : $7\frac{1}{2}/9$ b.h.p. ; *PETROL* : 70 b.h.p.
C.I. (Diesel Oil) : From 18 to 130 b.h.p.

JOHN I. THORNYCROFT & CO., LIMITED, THORNYCROFT HOUSE, LONDON, S.W.1

YACHTING MONTHLY

MOTOR & CRUISING

The YACHTING MONTHLY has been for 40 years the practical sailing man's magazine. It is edited and published by people who have their own boats; its articles and designs are selected to interest the owner of the dinghy, sharpie, weekend cruiser or ocean racer. Its regular features include descriptions of yachts and their gear, cruising, racing designs and "gadgets." It costs **25s. a year,** post free to any part of the world. Published on the 1st of each month.

3 & 4, CLEMENTS INN, STRAND, LONDON, W.C.2

FAIREY
MARINE
LIMITED

FAIREY MARINE LTD. is a subsidiary of the world-famous Fairey Aviation Co. Ltd., and has been formed for the specific purpose of specialising in the most advanced types of boats and equipment, including mast and hull construction, at Hamble.

FAIREY MARINE LTD · HAYES · MIDDLESEX

Perfection by Evolution

THE KITTIWAKE
(Rissa Tridactyla Tridactyla)

The Kittiwake, although the smallest of the true gulls has the greatest staying power, and has followed ships the whole way across the Atlantic. It is, in fact, a creature of the sea and the winds, evolved to its present perfection of air and seaworthiness through countless generations from the primeval pterodactyl.

The British Seagull outboard is also a product of evolution, designed by engineers, who are seamen as well, to fill the needs of seamen. During the fourteen years it has been on the market it has been continually improved and goes on improving. Perfection would be a nonsensical claim but we do say it is the best outboard motor in the world.

THE YACHTSMAN
SAIL AND POWER

OLD HARRY and the coastal scenes of casual cruising are the subjects of many articles and pictures in THE YACHTSMAN. The magazine is published quarterly and contains authoritative contributions on every aspect of the sport, including racing, dinghies and power craft. It is printed on art paper and is well illustrated with many fine photographs and designs.

Subscription: **8/6d.** per annum post free, to all parts of the world.

Established 1891.　Governing Director and Editor : K. Adlard Coles.

THE YACHTSMAN
ROLLS HOUSE,
2, BREAMS BUILDINGS,
LONDON, E.C.4.

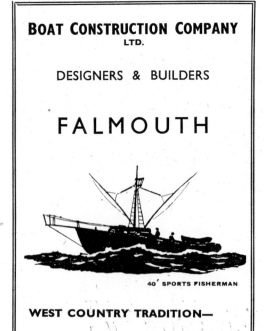

Tribute to Enterprise....

..Miss Britain III

Vindication of many then-revolutionary principles of Hubert Scott-Paine came with the success of Miss Britain III, the first boat to attain 100 miles per hour on salt-water which crowned many years' work by its designer. Much more remained to be done, but this famous boat's triumph marked a big 'leap ahead.' It resulted in the eventual countering of enemy light coastal forces by High-Speed Hard Chine craft—envisaged by Hubert Scott-Paine a decade before war came and developed by him for Britain, Canada and America. So much is owed to one man's perspicacity. The same Scott-Paine pattern of personal initiative and painstaking practical application of his theories has contributed much towards the famous M.T.B.'s, M.G.B.'s and Rescue Launches ; High Speed Craft serving Marine Aircraft and Port and River Authorities ; also new types for the Private Owner.

GOOD BOATS WITHIN EVERYMAN'S MEANS

THE reason for the very low price of these boats is the VEE-ROOT slimstrake method of construction. This is an adaptation of traditional methods of building which lends itself to planned production and saves waste of material and labour. At the same time it gives a stronger boat and does not restrict the designer in laying down his lines or the ordinary boatbuilder in carrying out adaptations and repairs.

PRAM DINGHIES. P.2. L.O.A. 6 ft., beam 3 ft. 6 in., M.D. 1 ft. 4 in., double skin of ⅛-in. thick, painted spruce, weight approx. 78 lbs.
£21 10s. 0d. plus tax

P.6. L.O.A. 8 ft., beam 3 ft. 9 in., M.D. 1 ft. 6 in., double skin of ⅛-in. thick, varnished mahogany, weight approx. 102 lbs.   £30 15s. 0d. plus tax

SAILING PRAMS. T.P.11. L.O.A. 8 ft. 9 in., beam 4 ft., M.D. 1 ft. 7 in., double skin of ¼ in. painted spruce, weight approx. 118 lbs. £29 0s. 0d.

S.P.1012. Spruce mast and rigging with balanced lug sail, 45 sq. ft. and rudder for above.
£21 15s. 0d.

SAILING DINGHIES. D.14. L.O.A. 10 ft., beam 4 ft. 6 in., M.D. 1 ft. 10 in., single skin, of ¼ in. painted spruce fitted with steel centre-board, weight approx 195 lbs.   £31 10s. 0d.

S.D.17. As above complete with mast and rigging, with balanced lug sail 60 sq. ft. and rudder, weight approx. 245 lbs.   £56 0s. 0d.

S.D.19. As above, double skin ⅛-in. thick, varnished mahogany, weight approx. 266 lbs.
£71 10s. 0d.

H.S.20. L.O.A. 10 ft., beam 4 ft. 3 in., M.D. 2ft., double skin of ⅜-in. thick, varnished mahogany, mast and rigging with balanced lug sail 60 sq. ft. and rudder, weight approx. 370 lbs. £75 0s. 0d.

OUTBOARD MOTORBOATS. O.B.23. L.O.A. 12 ft., beam 4 ft. 6 in., M.D. 1 ft. 7 in., transom 1 ft. 5 in. deep, double skin of ⅜-in. thick, varnished mahogany, weight approx. 175 lbs.
£41 5s. 0d.

RACING DINGHIES. N.34. (*Naiad* one-design). L.O.A. 12 ft. with hinged mast lowered on winch, Bermudian rig, 80 sq. ft., double skin of ⅛-in. thick, spruce hull, varnished interior, painted exterior, weight approx. 160 lbs.
£125 0s. 0d.

MOTOR DINGHIES. M.B. 35. (V.R. Safety dinghy). L.O.A. 12 ft., beam 5 ft. 3 in., M.D. 2 ft. 3½ in., level midship thwart housing 2¾ h.p. "Norman" air-cooled engine Type T.300. Complete specification on request.
£250 0s. 0d.

DELIVERY DATES. At the time of going to press the following delays elapse between receipt of order and delivery. Prams 4-5 weeks. Pulling dinghies fitted with centre-board and canoes 5-6 weeks. Outboard motor boats 6-7 weeks. Sailing dinghies 7-8 weeks.

* *The prices quoted above allow a trade discount to other boat builders, stores, etc., and you will be doing your boatbuilder a service if you order through him. We do, however, accept direct orders.*

EXPORT AGENTS.   APPLICATIONS ARE INVITED FOR AGENCIES OVERSEAS

BUSS & ELSTON LTD.,
COLE KINGS, HAGDEN LANE, WATFORD, HERTS.

Yachting World

THE LEADING YACHTING JOURNAL

All who enjoy sailing or motor-cruising on sea or inland waters find the "Yachting World" full of absorbing interest. Attractively produced and brightly illustrated, it continues to provide news, comments and up-to-date authorative information of value both to beginner and expert. Whether you are interested in power or sail "Yachting World" is a most valuable companion and guide.

"YACHTING WORLD" (Published Monthly 1/6) is one of the twenty-nine Technical, Trade and Specialised Journals produced by Associated Iliffe Press, Dorset House, Stamford Street, London, S.E.1

"No stir in the air — No stir in the sea"

YACHTSMEN who experience the sort of conditions which prevailed when "Sir Ralph the Rover" was in his destructive mood, probably feel just as resentful as he when becalmed, but there would be no occasion with a PARSONS engine installed for auxiliary power.

PARSONS

10 to 150 h.p. PETROL OR KEROSENE

"THEY NEVER LET YOU DOWN"

THE PARSONS ENGINEERING CO. LTD.
—— SOUTHAMPTON ——

PHONE: 2727-8   'GRAMS: "PARSENGCO"

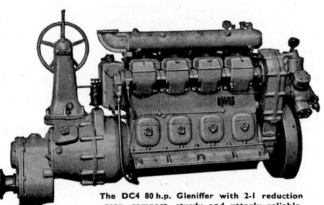

"What's the Weather Report? Our Wireless has broken down."
"Gale Warning! — We've got a 'Schooner Set'—*Built for the job.*"

SCHOONER SETS   51a St. MARY STREET, BRIDGWATER, SOM.

S-L Equipment has long been recognised as standard equipment for all pleasure craft, the reliability and efficiency of which was proved, during the war, by the fact that S-L supplied the needs of the Royal Navy.

We are endeavouring to meet requirements for Yacht equipment through the trade. Keep in touch with your boatbuilder for the latest information about deliveries of S-L Equipment.

SIMPSON-LAWRENCE LTD
St. Kentigern Works, St. Andrews Sq., Glasgow C.1
Phone: Bel. 0801   Grams: "Afloat," Glasgow

ROBERT ROSS
YACHTING BOOKS

LET'S GO CRUISING.

By Eric C. Hiscock.

In this book Mr. Hiscock writes in a light and entertaining manner about the practical side of cruising ; the different yachts, the advantages and disadvantages of their rigs, gear and fittings ; of seamanship and heavy weather ; of pilotage, navigation and cruising grounds.

With more than fifty half-tone illustrations and thirteen line drawings.   2nd. Edition **9/6**d net.

*

SAILING DAYS.

By K. Adlard Coles.

" This very attractive book is like a gleam of sunshine on a dull day. . . . the practiced pen of the author imparts life to Channel cruising and to races such as that " Round the Island," while the very excellent photographs recall vividly the old haunts . . . " Sir Alker Tripp in *Yachting Monthly*   Fifth Edition **8/6**d net.

*

CRUISING YACHTS : DESIGN AND PERFORMANCE.

By T. Harrison Butler, A.I.N.A.

This book covers the whole subject of yacht designing including the theory of hull balance, from the first rough sketch to the completed drawing and specification. Into it is woven much practical knowledge of little ships and the details which contribute to comfort and sea-worthiness.

With fifty-one drawings and complete plans of some of the author's most successful designs.   2nd, Edition **15s.** net.

*

SOUTH AND EAST.

By Henry Rooke.

A particularly readable account of sailing experiences aboard a converted trawler in all sorts of weather, and ocean racing in a yacht across the North Sea. **7/6**d net.

*

IMMORTAL SAILS.

By Lt.-Col. Henry Hughes.

The story of the rise and fall of the trade of Portmadoc and the ships associated with it. Illustrated with photographs of many famous sailing vessels. **15s.** net.

The Publishers are always pleased to consider MSS on nautical subjects, preferably highly illustrated.

ROBERT ROSS & CO., LTD.
ROLLS HOUSE
2 Breams Buildings, LONDON, E.C.4